WINNING
HORSE RACE
BETTING SYSTEMS

DAVID DUNCAN

foulsham
LONDON • NEW YORK • TORONTO • SYDNEY

foulsham

The Oriel, Thames Valley Court, 183-187 Bath Road,
Slough, Berkshire SL1 4AA, England

ISBN 978-0-572-03574-7

A CIP record for this book is available from the British Library

Printed and bound in the UK by CPI Mackays, Chatham ME5 8TD

CONTENTS

✳

INTRODUCTION

The definitive guide to betting on horses has never been written, and in all probability never will be. The sport of racing thoroughbreds in Britain is so complex and so diverse that over any reasonable period of time the results of races cannot be predicted with a sufficient degree of accuracy to guarantee consistent profits for even the most knowledgeable of backers. In addition, with the experience of over a century and a half of organised betting behind them, the bookmakers of today are so professional in their approach to odds-making for a multi-million pound industry, that the punter, however skilled, will always be at something of a disadvantage.

All that said, I believe it is no idle boast to claim that this book is the most comprehensive short treatise on racing and betting that has ever appeared in print. My intimate association with the sport goes back nearly 40 years, so I can examine every aspect of it from a betting point of view and I hope I have communicated it in a clear and concise way that beginners as well as seasoned enthusiasts will find easy to follow. This in-depth analysis is designed to help the reader get the best from a pastime which will obviously be more pleasurable if they can contrive a profit from it.

Beginning with single selections, the first half of the book is devoted to the difficult and controversial subject of staking correctly, and incorporates an appreciation of the much-vaunted concept of 'value' in relation to chance. It then moves from level stakes to sophisticated methods of regulating them in such a way as to maximise the potential for financial gain. There are chapters on racing permutations for single selections and on ways of combining bets on more than one horse in a race, either to increase the possibility of a really big win from multiple selections or to achieve steadier profits by making a punters' 'book' against the bookmakers in order to beat them at their own game.

I look at selection procedures too in great detail, backed up by statistics providing readers with valuable knowledge unavailable elsewhere, as well as expertise, much of which they could probably never hope to acquire by trial and error. There is also a section giving complete details of a number of fully automatic racing systems which have been tried and tested over many years and which have the potential to win again in the seasons to come.

My tour through the betting jungle concludes with a discussion of overall betting strategy, supported by a set of indicators that will nearly always point in the right direction in a given set of circumstances and, almost as important, steer the unwary away from the many pitfalls which lie in wait for anyone who bets on horses. The Golden Rules for betting exchanges in particular are written with a view to alerting the average racing enthusiast to the dangers so prevalent on the exchanges, where professional 'traders' and racing insiders may well have an unfair advantage.

It is never possible to remove the element of gambling from the sport entirely, and no one would want that to happen. There is, of course, no such thing as a racing certainty. For this reason no one should ever stake more than they can reasonably afford to lose on their opinions about horse racing contests, whether independently formed or arrived at by following the advice given in these pages.

Traditionally, racing, and betting in particular, have been seen as male preserves. In fact this was never entirely the case and nowadays it is definitely not so. Women are involved at all levels in every racing activity; this includes the very large numbers of female punters who try to make their betting pay as a way of enhancing their interest in the sport. This book, therefore, is addressed to them as much as to men, and is written in the belief that all will find it equally instructive and, hopefully, profitable.

David Duncan

1

Stake Right, Lose Less and Win More

Variable Stakes – The Pitfalls

A well-known professional gambler once remarked that it is not how many winners you back that counts in the end, but how you stake on them. If you think about it, this must be right, for unless the punter's strike rate of winners is so low as to be virtually hopeless in the long term, the chance of a profit will always be determined by what is bet on successful nominations in relation to the stakes on losers.

This is a truism that has probably not occurred to a lot of punters, however long they have been at the game. Take for example this rota of bets:

Four Horses: £10 staked.

£4	6–4	Lost
£5	7–2	Lost
50p	7–1	Won
50p	7–1	Won

For whatever reason, the backer has decided that their strongest preference among the four horses is for the one at the second-best odds. But what is the outcome? For their total outlay of £10 the backer receives only £8 in return, a LOSS of £2 overall.

Yet if the £10 stake had been divided equally between the four horses, there would have been a PROFIT of no less than £30! Incredible, but bookmakers receive bets like these in large quantities every racing day.

Does this mean that level stakes are always the best? Not necessarily, although it must be said right from the start that it will always be the safest method of staking for any punter, big or small, to adopt. And this is for the simple reason that having the same amount on each selection is a sure way of avoiding the catastrophic mishit mirrored in the foregoing example. With an equal distribution on each selection of the total amount bet over a given period, at least backers receive full credit for the winners they back, even if they have to accept that all their losers will have the same weight in the final reckoning.

The problem with level stakes, especially from the point of view of the ordinary punter betting in relatively small amounts, is that in racing it can be very difficult to build up a reasonable gain, even over a lengthy period. Take someone who is regularly able to find, say, 40 per cent of winners from all the horses backed, but at an average price of only 6–4. This will do no better than break even overall, despite a very respectable score of winning selections.

Finding a way out of this conundrum is a huge problem. Either the backer must somehow increase the ratio of winners to losers, with the risk of a reduction in the average starting price, or must back horses at better prices, thereby risking a drop in the percentage of winners. An attempt to strike the right balance could easily upset the apple cart, which would result in doing worse than before.

The other problem with level stakes is one of betting psychology as much as anything. Since they offer neither a quick road to profit nor an easy escape route when things go wrong, they are not very exciting. Turning a successful run into a spectacular gain, assuming the run is continued, is always going to be a lengthy process. Equally, once a losing run sets in, there is bound to be a long, hard road back from the financial red to black, even if the number of winners improves dramatically.

Little wonder therefore that most punters, even if they accept the general notion of staking roughly the same on each horse in line with their betting means, still like to vary the amounts of their bets according to the strength of their convictions about this or that selection.

Let us take another example of variable staking on a series of bets covering four horses. In this case there is a strong possibility that the backer has allowed stakes to be determined by the prices of selections rather than by his or her own judgement of relative chances.

Four Horses: £10 staked.

£5	6–4	Lost
£3	7–2	Lost
£1.50	8–1	Lost
50p	10–1	Won

This time there were three losers offset by a 10–1 winner, yielding an overall LOSS of £4.50. However, had the £10 been split equally between the four horses with bets of £2.50 on each, the outcome would have been a PROFIT of £17.50. Not quite the debacle of the first example, but bad enough.

No doubt anyone making this wager would argue in their own defence, after the event at least, that they fancied the 6–4 shot much more than the rest, hence the large stake on that animal. This is all very well if the selection criteria, whatever they might have been, had genuinely indicated that the horse at 6–4 was indeed the best bet, and that the others had lesser chances commensurate with the amount bet on them. For many punters it is much more likely that the stakes were fixed, not by any objective measure of relative chance but, solely according to the probable odds for each, with the bigger stakes on the shorter prices.

Value in Betting – The Illusion

This belief that the 'market', whether on the racecourse or in the shape of a newspaper betting forecast, will nearly always be right, colours the thinking behind many people's attitude to staking. To rid the mind of this conviction is certainly not easy, and this brings us to the concept of 'value' which embraces a different and, in some ways, opposite view of how the betting market should determine stakes.

Value has been the buzz word among the betting fraternity since the 1990s. Anyone who consistently finds value in the odds of the horses backed, we are told, must have a better chance of winning over a period of time than someone who is content to accept any old price about a fancied animal.

This is all very well, but how is value to be assessed? Racing is an 'opinion' sport when it comes to betting, and whether or not the price about a particular runner represents something-for-nothing is just as much a matter of opinion as the wide variety of views different people will frequently take over the possible outcome of a given race. No one has yet discovered an accurate measure of odds in relation to true chance or, if they have, they are keeping it to themselves and for very good reasons. Plenty of theories have been aired, for which big claims have been made, but in practice, in the hard world of the modern betting industry, value is an elusive, perhaps even an illusory, concept. Everyone wants to back a true 3–1 chance at 8–1 but this is rarely possible. Professional bookmakers and odds-makers are just not in the business of making mistakes of this kind.

This fact is well illustrated if practically any horse race is analysed according to the method of converting odds to percentages used by the bookmakers themselves in framing the odds for races. Just one example at this point will serve to make the realities of the situation clear.

On the next page are the runners and prices for a recent renewal of the Ribblesdale Stakes, an important race for three-year-old fillies run each June at the Royal Ascot meeting. There were nine horses in the field, so each of them had a mathematical 8–1 chance of winning, and this is shown in the table immediately to the right of the runners, but expressed as a percentage:

$100 \div (8 + 1) = 11.1$ per cent to the nearest 0.1 per cent.

The next column shows the actual price of each horse similarly converted to a percentage, for example:

Ocean Silk at 7–2; $100 \div (3.5 + 1) = 22.2$ per cent.

The last two columns reveal by how much the available odds differ in percentage terms from the real mathematical chance, either to the bookmakers' or backer's advantage as the case may be. With Ocean Silk the real odds are 8–1 against in purely mathematical terms, but the bookmaker offers only 7–2, an 11.1 per cent advantage in his favour.

On the other hand, with Inchberry at 12–1, the backer has the advantage this time, one of 3.4 per cent, which represents the difference between the available odds and the real chance of 8–1.

Even in a race which according to the bookmakers was a fairly open affair (Spanish Sun eventually triumphed with Ocean Silk and Mezzo Soprano in the minor places), clearly all the value lies not with the backers but with the bookmakers. Only about half the field had a sound chance of succeeding, and in five cases out of nine the odds are in their favour. Humouresque, with a 1.1 per cent advantage to the backer, arguably represents a slight chink in the bookmakers' armour, but really the punters are left with the 'edge' just or the 'rags' which could only win in the

**RIBBLESDALE STAKES – MATHEMATICAL
PROBABILITIES AND ADVANTAGES FROM QUOTED ODDS**

Odds	Horse	Mathematical probability %	Odds converted to probability %	Bookmakers' advantage %	Backer's advantage %
7–2	OCEAN SILK	11.1	22.2	11.1	
4–1	SUMMITVILLE	11.1	20.0	8.9	
9–2	SPANISH SUN	11.1	18.2	7.1	
11–2	SUN ON THE SEA	11.1	15.4	4.3	
6–1	MEZZO SOPRANO	11.1	14.3	3.2	
9–1	HUMOURESQUE	11.1	10.0		1.1
12–1	INCHBERRY	11.1	7.7		3.4
33–1	MOONSPRITE	11.1	2.9		8.2
66–1	LADIES DAY	11.1	1.5		9.6
		99.9	112.2	34.6	22.3
			–99.9	–22.3	
			Over-round = 12.3	12.3	

Note: the 0.1 per cent overall shortfall against the 100 per cent to which the mathematical probability should aggregate is due to the rounding down of the percentages for each horse to one place after the decimal point.

event of a major, virtually unpredictable, form upset. In other words, if the layers' assessment of the race is no better than approximately correct, the market has been framed in such a way that there is hardly any value anywhere for the backer. In the event, the four horses in the race whose odds were to the backer's advantage occupied the last four places home.

It is a sad fact of betting life that the above scenario is typical of the betting market on the vast majority of races, day in, day out, week in, week out. Only when a runner has been seriously underestimated, which happens rarely, does the informed or inspired backer have the opportunity to apply the concept of value profitably.

All this shows just what backers are up against in their search for a profit. It is very difficult to nullify, let alone reverse, the bookmakers' trading margin on any race, but there is one simple measure which sensible punters can take to protect themselves to some extent. This is to bet only in relatively small fields. A glance at the two races for which the full rota of odds are set out below should be enough to hammer home this vital point. Both events took place at a recent Glorious Goodwood meeting.

STEWARDS' CUP

Odds	Horse	Odds converted to probability %
7–2	FIRE UP THE BAND	22.2
4–1	PATAVELLIAN	20.0
7–1	FAYR JAG	12.5
9–1	MUTAWAQED	10.0
12–1	ONLYTIME WILL TELL	7.7
14–1	ENDLESS SUMMER	6.7
16–1	COLONEL COTTON	5.9
16–1	LOYAL TYCOON	5.9
20–1	GOOD GIRL	4.8
25–1	ABBAJABBA	3.8
25–1	BUDELLI	3.8
25–1	FRIZZANTE	3.8
33–1	HALMAHERA	2.9
33–1	PIC UP STICKS	2.9
33–1	TOM TUN	2.9
33–1	TRACE CLIP	2.9
40–1	COMPTON DRAGON	2.4
40–1	FUNFAIR WANE	2.4
40–1	IDLE POWER	2.4
40–1	PIETER BRUEGHEL	2.4
50–1	BANJO BAY	2.0
66–1	BOND BECKS	1.5
66–1	MATERIAL WITNESS	1.5
66–1	MY AMERICAN BEAUTY	1.5

66–1	PLATEAU	1.5
66–1	PRINCE CYRANO	1.5
66–1	SIMIANNA	1.5
66–1	STEEL BLUE	1.5
66–1	VANDERLIN	1.5
		142.3

GORDON STAKES

Odds	Horse	Odds converted to probability %
4–1	LET ME TRY AGAIN	20.0
9–2	HIGH ACCOLADE	18.2
9–2	SALSALINO	18.2
11–2	DUBAI SUCCESS	15.4
7–1	HAWK FLYER	12.5
12–1	PHOENIX REACH	7.7
14–1	UNIGOLD	6.7
16–1	GOLD MEDALLIST	5.9
25–1	WAVERTREE BOY	3.8
50–1	TITUREL	2.0
		110.4

A comparison of the over-round in these two races reveals the trap which the bookmakers habitually lay for inexperienced punters, as well as informed ones whose knowledge of betting mathematics is not always all it should be. Although all the odds for the Stewards' Cup, a very big handicap with many runners, look generous, both in terms of prices for individual contenders and as a whole, in fact they are no such thing. The over-round on the race is high at 42.3 per cent. In the 10-runner Gordon Stakes on the other hand, layers competing for business in the Ring have been unable to hide their lack of generosity behind a big field with lots of fancied candidates. In this race their margin is low at 10.4 per cent, a huge difference compared with 42.3 per cent.

Generally speaking, at meetings where the market is not as strong as at Glorious Goodwood, two per cent for each runner in a race will aggregate to the over-round to which bookmakers can be expected to bet, up to a maximum of about 35 per cent. In small fields, therefore, there is much greater value for the punter. Apparently 'tasty' prices in races with a lot of runners, especially handicaps, are a snare and a delusion. Apart from serious errors by the bookmakers which are as scarce as taxis on a wet night, without exception every runner in a small field offers better value, whatever its price. Beyond that, this author would not care to speculate when it comes to trying to establish a value system by which the price on offer for a horse can be compared to its real chance on form.

Others have tried and failed. Modern British ideas about value are similar to the long-standing American concept of 'overlays' which attempt, by an independent assessment of chances, to discover in *pari-mutuel* pools, horses standing at odds significantly better than a price which would reflect their true prospect of winning.

There are no legal bookmakers in the USA. So with overlays the theory is that errors in *mutuel* odds can be exploited profitably because the prices for the horses most favoured by the betting fraternity, the 'public plays', frequently over-estimate the chance of these short-priced animals relative to less-fancied horses at longer odds. This is borne out by the actual results of races. Form only works out some of the time. Consequently the *mutuel* odds against candidates largely ignored by the public often represent real value. If the so-called overlay on a particular horse is high enough, a bet is justified. Thus odds, not selection criteria, determine what is to be backed. The overlay operator will more often than not be required to support one horse in a race even if, in his personal opinion, another horse is more likely to win.

The overlay concept is not necessarily one which

concentrates exclusively on outsiders, however, though that is its tendency. Favourites or near-favourites can be 'under-bet' as well as 'over-bet', and the former would constitute an overlay worthy of exploiting if the price difference compared with the estimated real chance is considered significant enough.

The overlay system may or may not work in the USA. Some extravagant boasts have been made about its successes over the years, though if the idea is really so brilliant, it is not unfair to ask why every American horse-player worth his overlay salt has not long since forsaken the tracks for a life of luxury and ease in some tropical paradise. Be that as it may, in a British context, backing horses for no other reason than that they are thought to be at odds greater than their true form chance seems a suspect proposition.

As we have already noted, British bookmakers make depressingly few mistakes. Any racing enthusiast would surely agree about that. As for Tote prices in this country, they tend to follow, fairly closely, the market established by the bookmakers. True, outsiders on the Tote usually better the bookies' price, but out of the large number of outsiders on every card, how many win?

Whether betting with the bookmakers or on the Tote, judgements about value have to be made before the start of a race. Just because a horse is at a higher price than it should be, in the backer's estimation, does not mean that it will actually succeed. Even if you can regularly spot what you believe to be significant discrepancies in the odds, the difference still has to be translated into what really matters, namely winners.

If racing is compared to a purely mathematical game like roulette, then a competent player should win against the House in the long run if only they had a mathematical advantage in the odds, just as in reality the casinos make their money from the 'edge' they build into the odds in their own favour. In racing, the bookmakers' edge, as explained earlier, usually varies between around 10 per cent and 35 per cent on the total number of runners in a race. Can a 'value' system for single selections really offset this degree of disadvantage to the backer?

Realistically, a horse strongly fancied at a price which seems fair is probably the best that serious backers of horses can do, and the right price comes down to personal judgement in the end, not a magic formula. Much more important is to find methods of regularly backing a lot of winners. By contrast, backing strings of horses by price alone, even if the punter has no great faith in their ability to win, is a pill that is not easy to swallow.

This opening chapter sets the tone for the rest of the book. Racing is a hard school and making money from it will always be an uphill struggle. That does not mean that it cannot be done. In racing, as in life, there are ways and means of overcoming most difficulties. So read on.

2
Staking Plans

Graduated Stakes Systems

The aim of all staking plans is to arrange matters so that big stakes go on to winners and small stakes on to losers, the opposite scenario to the examples of bad staking given in Chapter 1. The problem is that the pattern of winners and losers in any sequence can never be known in advance. And, despite the best efforts of all manner of mathematicians and statisticians down the years, no one has ever discovered a way of regulating stakes according to some fixed principle that will accommodate every possible pattern. However, this much is certain mathematically: a staking system on single selections must be based on one or other of two opposite ideas – either it increases after losers or after winners – although it is possible to combine both in one unified method of stakes regulation.

Where there is an increase after losers, the hope is that when a winner is found the stakes will have risen sufficiently to wipe out any losses on the sequence so far and to yield a profit overall. There are two problems here. First, when a winner occurs its price in relation to the stake on it might not be good enough to achieve this dual objective. Second, when a losing run is struck, and there will always be losing runs however sound the method of selection, even apparently modest increases have a tendency to produce a high level of staking very rapidly, thereby inevitably straining the backer's nerve and cash resources to the absolute limit. Given infinite quantities of these two latter assets, it is theoretically possible, as we shall soon see later, for increases always to turn losses into gains, but in practice the random factor in the incidence of winners to losers is extremely difficult to overcome.

On the other hand, when stakes are increased only after winners, many of the above objections no longer apply. Now the backer is not chasing losses but attempting to finance his/her betting with money from the bookmaker. Profits will mount on a winning run and stakes can be made to drop back quickly to an acceptable level in anticipation of a sequence of losers.

There is, however, a snag, and a big one at that. Examine the two sequences below on the supposition that there is a one-point increase after a winner and an immediate decrease to one point after a loser.

Lost, Won 2–1, Won Evens, Won Evens, Won 3–1, Lost, Lost, Lost

The results of the staking plan are:

| –1 | +2 | +2 | +3 | +12 | 5 | –1 | –1 |

There is an 11-point profit overall, compared with one of only three points at level stakes.

However, if the sequence is rearranged as follows, the staking plan does much less well.

Won 2–1, Lost, Won Evens, Lost, Won Evens, Lost, Won 3–1, Lost

Now the outcome is:

| +2 | –2 | +1 | –2 | +1 | –2 | +3 | –2 |

This time there is a loss of one point on a series with exactly the same number of winners and losers.

What all this means is that it is not only the number of winners to losers and the starting prices of winners that matters. Almost as important is the way in which winners fall. Systems like the above calling for increases after winners do best when successful selections occur, for the most part, in consecutive sequence, and the longer such sequences are, the better. Even with short-priced selections likely to give a good percentage of winners, however, there is no guarantee that this is a general pattern which will actually occur.

This point is reinforced if increasing after losers is examined in more detail, for here also the backer is gambling on a favourable pattern where the largest stakes will go on winners, not losers.

Let us suppose that stakes are to be increased by one point after each loser and decreased by one point after a winner. This is the result of the first sequence set out on the previous page:

Lost, Won 2–1, Won Evens, Won Evens, Won 3–1, Lost, Lost, Lost
  –1   +4   +1   +1   +3   –1   –2   –3

This amounts to a two-point gain against the three points at level stakes.

But look what happens on the second sequence:

Won 2–1, Lost, Won Evens, Lost, Won Evens, Lost, Won 3–1, Lost
  +2   –1   +2   –1   +2   –1   +6   –1

This time there is a gain of eight points, a much better result.

However, if the original pattern is rearranged for a second time, the same system of staking produces a complete reversal in the backer's fortunes:

Won 2–1, Won Evens, Won Evens, Won 3–1, Lost, Lost, Lost, Lost
  +2   +1   +1   +3   –1   –2   –3   –4

Now there is no profit at all, but a loss of three points.

Lengthen any of the above sequences to mirror an

actual extended period of betting, and the variations in what any staking plan can achieve will become even more apparent. Everything depends, ultimately, on pattern, and the incidence of winners will not always be such as to allow a system of staking to maximise profits or minimise losses. It may do so but, then again, it may not. This is for the simple reason that how winners fall in relation to losers is an unknown at the time betting begins.

All this is emphasised tenfold if extremes of the two types of staking are considered. One is the Reverse Monte Carlo, also known as the Reverse Labouchère system. The other is generally known as 'cover-to-win' or 'retrieve' staking. They are included in this chapter because the author, in his capacity as a reader of racing and betting manuscripts for a well-known publishing house, has seen both plans hailed frequently over as 'infallible systems' – the ultimate answer to the problem of beating the bookmaker.

Cover-to-win System

'Cover-to-win' staking takes the principle of increasing stakes after losers to its absolute limit. In its simplest form the method is to back each selection in a series to win a fixed amount. This will always be the sum of any losses so far plus the intended profit from the coup as a whole. After the first loser one adds one's loss on to the original target-profit figure and then increases the stake on the next bet according to the odds available, in order to achieve the new target figure should the horse win. Betting continues in this manner until a winner occurs, thereby winning back the accumulated deficit as well as producing the desired profit on the coup.

According to its protagonists, the system works because it is the only way of achieving the seemingly impossible. It does actually succeed in guaranteeing that the largest stake in a series must fall on a winner, and in such a way that inevitably a profit is bound to accrue.

This all sounds deceptively easy and the most deceptive thing about it is that for a lot of the time it succeeds, provided bets are confined to the type of selection which can be expected to yield a good percentage of winners without worrying too much about starting prices. But take for example the following series of bets where five losers and a single winner at short odds represent a very low level of success in punting terms. Like all the examples in Chapter 2, the stakes are exact to the nearest 1p so that the method can be followed in detail. In practice, when actually placing bets with a bookmaker, odd amounts would have to be rounded up or down to the nearest 5p or 10p.

COVER-TO-WIN SYSTEM – EXAMPLE 1

Target	Price	Stake	Result	Profit	Loss	Accumulated Profit (+) or Loss (−)
£10.00	3–1	£3.33	Lost		£3.33	−£3.33
£13.33	7–2	£3.81	Lost		£3.81	−£7.14
£17.14	6–1	£2.86	Lost		£2.86	−£10.00
£20.00	3–1	£6.67	Lost		£6.67	−£16.67
£26.67	2–1	£13.34	Lost		£13.34	−£30.01
£40.01	11–8	£29.10	Won	£40.01		+£10.00

Everything is fine. Whereas there would have been a hefty loss at level stakes on the sequence, the cover-to-win formula has actually achieved its objective of a £10 gain, and this without too much betting capital being placed at risk.

However, if the next example is studied closely, it becomes apparent that terrific problems can occur on a less favourable series of bets:

COVER-TO-WIN SYSTEM – EXAMPLE 2

Target	Price	Stake	Result	Profit	Loss	Accumulated Profit (+) or Loss (−)
£10.00	13–8	£6.15	Lost		£6.15	−£6.15
£16.15	7–4	£9.23	Lost		£9.23	−£15.38
£25.38	4–5	£31.73	Lost		£31.73	−£47.11
£57.11	3–1	£19.04	Lost		£19.04	−£66.15
£76.15	Evens	£76.15	Lost		£76.15	−£142.30
£152.30	3–1	£50.77	Lost		£50.77	−£193.07
£203.07	2–1	£101.54	Lost		£101.54	−£294.61
£304.61	4–6	£456.92	Lost		£456.92	−£751.53
£761.53	4–5	£951.91	Won	£761.53		+£10.00

True, the backer has made the £10, but at what risk? On a sequence of only nine bets it has been necessary to stake a total of £1703.44 to win what, by comparison, is the trivial amount of £10. Cover-to-win staking embroiled the backer in a capital outlay completely out of proportion to the expected gain.

There are two reasons for this. First, the losing run has extended beyond just a handful of bets and second, every time a horse at odds-on is to be backed, the stake jumps to a dizzy height. 'Very well,' says the cover-to-win enthusiast, 'the problem is quite easily solved – there is no bet if the selection starts at odds-on.' But the trouble with this is that as soon as the runners at the shortest prices are eliminated, the ratio of winners to losers could easily decrease, and the plan's other bugbear, an extended losing run, may decisively come into play, once again causing the stakes to spiral dangerously out of proportion.

Anyone inclined to reject these arguments on the grounds that they are based on an imaginary illustration should dip into the Form Book. Cover-to-win staking is almost always operated on favourites, but there are plenty of examples in the record of results where favourites run up long losing sequences. Take for example a recent big

August meeting at York. Here is the record of favourites over the three days, with the necessary stakes for cover-to-win £10 on each completed coup at the meeting.

COVER-TO-WIN SYSTEM – REALITY

Race No. Horse	Target	Price	Stake	Result	Profit	Loss	Accumulated Profit (+) or Loss (−)
Day One							
1 In Command	£10.00	8–11	£13.75	Lost		£13.75	−£13.75
2 Berlin Blue							
Private Song	£23.75	7–2	£6.79	Lost		£6.79	−£20.54
3 Halling	£30.54	6–4	£20.36	Won	£30.54		+£10.00
4 Royal Court	£10.00	11–4	£3.64	Lost		£3.64	−£3.64
5 Double							
Splendour	£13.64	4–1	£3.41	Lost		£3.41	−£7.05
6 Celeric	£17.05	9–4	£7.58	Won	£17.06		+£10.01
7 Demolition							
Man	£10.00	11–4	£3.64	Lost		£3.64	−£3.64
Day Two							
1 Swiss Coast	£13.64	3–1	£4.55	Lost		£4.55	−£8.19
2 Shamadara	£18.19	2–1	£9.10	Lost		£9.10	−£17.29
3 Harbour Dues							
Corradini	£27.29	7–1	£3.90	Lost		£3.90	−£21.19
4 The West	£31.19	2–1	£15.60	Lost		£15.60	−£36.79
5 Fahim	£46.79	7–4	£26.74	Lost		£26.74	−£63.53
6 Tipsy Creek	£73.53	6–4	£49.02	Lost		£49.02	−£112.55
7 Clan Chief							
Zalotti	£122.55	11–2	£22.28	Lost		£22.28	−£134.83
Day Three							
1 Elnadim	£144.83	11–8	£105.33	Lost		£105.33	−£240.16
2 Seeba	£250.16	11–4	£90.97	Lost		£90.97	−£331.13
3 Mind Games	£341.13	7–4	£194.93	Lost		£194.93	−£526.06
4 Intidab							
North Song	£536.06	11–2	£97.47	Lost		£97.47	−£623.53
5 Dacha	£633.53	11–2	£115.19	Lost		£115.19	−£738.72
6 Annaba	£748.72	3–1	£249.57	Lost		£249.57	−£988.29
7 Ali-Royal	£998.29	100–30	£299.49	Lost		£299.49	−£1287.78

This is a classic case of stakes getting completely out of control in a plan that increases after losers. The cover-to-win operator has won £10 twice, but lost £1287.78 in just three days at this York meeting. Even choosing correctly between the several joint favourites would not have helped, since they all lost.

However attractive in theory, cover-to-win staking is a fool's paradise. Most of the time it does win. Provided it is worked on selections which give a good percentage of winners overall, it goes merrily on its way producing small, but steady gains. Punters, lured into a false sense of security, shout 'Eureka!' and think that at last they have found the answer to their problem. A steady income from racing is there for the taking. But sooner or later the crash always comes. One disastrous losing run will destroy all the accumulated profits, stakes escalate to ridiculously high levels and the punter without unlimited financial means for betting is suddenly face to face with ruin.

The Reverse Labouchère System

Another staking plan often credited with near-magical properties is the Reverse Labouchère system borrowed from the world of the casino. In that context it has sometimes been operated with great success by syndicates working the even chances at roulette. As with all staking systems, a favourable pattern of results is essential if it is to deliver the goods. So, while most members of a roulette team playing the system will sit for hours winning a little or losing a little on balance, very occasionally one of them will strike a sequence that enables Reverse Labouchère to run up a huge profit very quickly. Needless to say, such syndicates are heavily discouraged by casino managements.

When used for betting on horses, it must be worked only on favourites offering the prospect of a high winning percentage, and the fact that a horse is likely to start at odds-on is no reason for excluding it. The system is one which calls for increases in stakes after winners. As we have seen, a large gain will only accrue from such systems if strings of consecutive, or near-consecutive, winners feature regularly in the pattern of results. Winners rather than prices are the most important consideration.

The system's rules can be summarised thus:

1 Write down a series of consecutive numbers from 1 upwards. For horse racing, 1 2 3 4 5 6 7 is recommended. This 'line' will be the initial arbiter of stakes and is adjusted after each bet.

2 Always stake the sum of the first and last number in the line. Cross these off after a loser, but add the winning stake to the end of the line after a winner.

3 If all the numbers in a line are eventually crossed off, start a new line of 1 to 7.

The effect of these rules is that stakes rise very sharply on a run of winners, but are cut back fairly gradually when losers are encountered. A high level of staking throughout is a characteristic of the plan.

The author has seen some very extravagant claims made for this plan over the years, and there is no doubt that a very handsome gain can be amassed very quickly on those occasions when the backer can do no wrong when it comes to selecting winners.

However, as a fair initial test for the plan, the sequence below has been constructed. From the 36 selections there are 15 winners and a level-stakes profit of 12.83 points. Despite the sound winning percentage, winners and losers tend to alternate fairly regularly. There are no long winning runs which we know in advance will help the plan to succeed.

REVERSE LABOUCHÈRE SYSTEM – EXAMPLE 1

Line	Stake	Result	Accumulated Profit (+) or Loss (−)
1 2 3 4 5 6 7	£8.00	Lost	−£8.00
~~1~~ 2 3 4 5 6 ~~7~~	£8.00	Lost	−£16.00
~~2~~ 3 4 5 ~~6~~	£8.00	Won 5–2	+£4.00
3 4 5 8	£11.00	Won 4–6	+£11.37
3 4 5 8 11	£14.00	Lost	−£2.63
~~3~~ 4 5 8 ~~11~~	£12.00	Lost	−£14.63
4 5 ~~8~~	£5.00	Lost	−£19.63
~~5~~ – 1 2 3 4 5 6 7	£8.00	Won 7–2	+£8.37
1 2 3 4 5 6 7 8	£9.00	Lost	−£0.63
~~1~~ 2 3 4 5 6 7 ~~8~~	£9.00	Lost	−£9.63
~~2~~ 3 4 5 6 ~~7~~	£9.00	Lost	−£18.63
~~3~~ 4 5 ~~6~~	£9.00	Won 11–8	−£6.21
4 5 9	£13.00	Won 9–4	+£23.04
4 5 9 13	£17.00	Won 3–1	+£74.04
4 5 9 13 17	£21.00	Lost	+£53.04
4 5 9 13 ~~17~~	£18.00	Lost	+£35.04
~~5~~ 9 ~~13~~	£9.00	Won 5–2	+£57.54
9 9	£18.00	Lost	+£39.54
~~9~~ ~~9~~ – 1 2 3 4 5 6 7	£8.00	Won 5–4	+£49.54
1 2 3 4 5 6 7 8	£9.00	Won 4–1	+£85.54
1 2 3 4 5 6 7 8 9	£10.00	Lost	+£75.54
~~1~~ 2 3 4 5 6 7 8 ~~9~~	£10.00	Lost	+£65.54
~~2~~ 3 4 5 6 7 ~~8~~	£10.00	Won 4–5	+£73.54
3 4 5 6 7 10	£13.00	Lost	+£60.54
~~3~~ 4 5 6 7 ~~10~~	£11.00	Lost	+£49.54
4 5 6 ~~7~~	£11.00	Lost	+£38.54
~~5~~ ~~6~~ – 1 2 3 4 5 6 7	£8.00	Won 9–4	+£56.54
1 2 3 4 5 6 7 8	£9.00	Lost	+£47.54
~~1~~ 2 3 4 5 6 7 ~~8~~	£9.00	Won 13–8	+£62.21
2 3 4 5 6 7 9	£11.00	Lost	+£51.21
~~2~~ 3 4 5 6 7 ~~9~~	£10.00	Lost	+£41.21
~~3~~ 4 5 6 ~~7~~	£10.00	Won 5–1	+£91.21
4 5 6 10	£14.00	Won 11–10	+£106.61
4 5 6 10 14	£18.00	Won 2–1	+£142.61
4 5 6 10 14 18	£22.00	Lost	+£120.61
4 5 6 10 14 ~~18~~	£19.00	Lost	+£101.61

At first glance a final gain of £101.61 looks a very fair outcome and seems to vindicate the system, even though there are no long winning runs which would have certainly spiralled stakes and profits in the space of only a few bets. On the other hand, the opening stake is one of £8, and if this is counted as one point, in level-stakes terms £8 × 12.83 points profit = £102.64 is much the same result.

On the next sequence, however, the real strengths, and also the weaknesses of Reverse Labouchère are much more evident.

REVERSE LABOUCHÈRE SYSTEM – EXAMPLE 2

Line	Stake	Result	Accumulated Profit (+) or Loss (–)
1 2 3 4 5 6 7	£8.00	Won 2–1	+£16.00
1 2 3 4 5 6 7 8	£9.00	Won 3–1	+£43.00
1 2 3 4 5 6 7 8 9	£10.00	Won 4–6	+£49.70
1 2 3 4 5 6 7 8 9 10	£11.00	Lost	+£38.70
~~1~~ 2 3 4 5 6 7 8 9 ~~10~~	£11.00	Lost	+£27.70
~~2~~ 3 4 5 6 7 8 ~~9~~	£11.00	Lost	+£16.70
~~3~~ 4 5 6 7 ~~8~~	£11.00	Won 6–4	+£33.20
4 5 6 7 11	£15.00	Won 2–1	+£63.20
4 5 6 7 11 15	£19.00	Won 11–10	+£84.10
4 5 6 7 11 15 19	£23.00	Lost	+£61.10
4 5 6 7 11 15 ~~19~~	£20.00	Won 1–2	+£71.10
5 6 7 11 15 20	£25.00	Won 4–7	+£85.35
5 6 7 11 15 20 25	£30.00	Won 4–6	+£105.45
5 6 7 11 15 20 25 30	£35.00	Won 6–4	+£157.95
5 6 7 11 15 20 25 30 35	£40.00	Won 11–8	+£213.15
5 6 7 11 15 20 25 30 35 40	£45.00	Lost	+£168.15
~~5~~ 6 7 11 15 20 25 30 35 ~~40~~	£41.00	Lost	+£127.15
~~6~~ 7 11 15 20 25 30 ~~35~~	£37.00	Lost	+£90.15
~~7~~ 11 15 20 25 ~~30~~	£36.00	Lost	+£54.15
~~11~~ 15 20 ~~25~~	£35.00	Lost	+£19.15
~~15 20~~ – 1 2 3 4 5 6 7	£8.00	Won 2–1	+£35.15

This sequence, although a relatively short one, tells us all that we need to know about the Reverse Labouchère system. Runs of three, three and five consecutive winners enable the plan to improve considerably on level stakes and it shows a marvellous gain of £213.15 after only 15 bets. But the fall from the heights is devastatingly sudden and swift. In the space of only five more bets, profits have dwindled to a mere £19.15!

Reverse Labouchère staking, therefore, must be operated with a predetermined 'check-out' point. On an opening stake of £8, a gain of £100 seems a reasonable goal. This should be set aside as an accumulated gain and the stake put back immediately to the original £8 as the starting point of a fresh coup, again with a target of £100. Anyone who cannot resist the temptation to go on betting past a reasonable check-out invariably runs a grave risk of seeing everything that has been gained dissipated in double-quick time.

With a £100 check-out on the above sequence, this would have been the excellent result:

REVERSE LABOUCHÈRE SYSTEM – EXAMPLE 3 WITH A CHECK-OUT

Line	Stake	Result	Accumulated Profit (+) or Loss (−)
5 6 7 11 15 20 25	£30.00	Won 4–6	+£105.45
1 2 3 4 5 6 7	£8.00	Won 6–4	+£12.00
1 2 3 4 5 6 7 8	£9.00	Won 11–8	+£24.42
1 2 3 4 5 6 7 8 9	£10.00	Lost	+£14.42
~~1~~ 2 3 4 5 6 7 8 ~~9~~	£10.00	Lost	+£4.42
~~2~~ 3 4 5 6 7 ~~8~~	£10.00	Lost	−£5.58
~~3~~ 4 5 6 ~~7~~	£10.00	Lost	−£15.58
4 5 ~~6~~	£5.00	Lost	−£20.58
~~5~~ – 1 2 3 4 5 6 7	£8.00	Won 2–1	−£4.58

Provided the check-out procedure is strictly observed, the author has no hesitation in saying that, on the right kind of selection, Reverse Labouchère is the best staking system he has ever encountered. Barring freak patterns of results, it is unlikely to worsen the level-stakes position by much, and on a favourable pattern can do much to improve it. It cannot be stressed enough, however, that the operator needs both a cool nerve and a highly disciplined attitude to betting if he/she is to get the best from the plan. One or two bets too many at the height of a successful run may be fatal, and any tendency to greed can be punished severely. It is also the height of folly to attempt to work the plan on anything but short-priced selections.

Level Stakes and Other Alternatives

It is fair to say that the backer can never go far wrong with level stakes, and that staking plans carry varying degrees of risk in addition to the normal factors of chance involved in selecting horses and betting on them.

One alternative to staking plans calling for the rigid regulation of stakes is to increase stakes generally for a period, if and when a worthwhile profit has accrued in the medium term. This calls for very sound judgement on the part of the backer, but may be the best hope of speeding up the process by which a worthwhile sum can be amassed with an equal amount bet on every horse. If profits continue to grow, the general level of staking can then be increased again when the time seems appropriate. Equally, should things go badly, a general adjustment in the opposite direction may tide the punter over a bad patch.

The racing enthusiast has choices in staking as in other areas of betting. Many will stand by level stakes, and there is an old maxim in racing that if a system cannot succeed at level stakes, then it cannot succeed at all. This is not strictly true. A staking plan can enhance profits but equally, the same plan may do worse than level stakes on a different and less favourable rota of results. Even a really sound staking method, for example Reverse Labouchère, can have its failures. This could be because of insufficient winners, the wrong pattern of results, or because the operator misjudges the situation and ends up losing all or most of what has been gained.

If level stakes are preferred in principle to formulae which vary the stakes from bet to bet, it is still possible to adjust the general level of staking in response to results. As an open-ended solution to the staking problem this has a lot of appeal but even here it is easy to make a mistake, for without foreknowledge the right time for a general increase or reduction in stakes will always be difficult to judge. When to take a good profit out of the betting continuum altogether and drop stakes back to something like their opening level is another imponderable that the backer is just as likely to get wrong as right. It will always be safer to cash in a big gain and start again, but in doing so greater profits still may be missed from playing up winnings should results continue to favour the punter.

There are, however, other options which, even if they are usually a great deal more hazardous, also offer the chance of much greater rewards in relation to outlay. These options are considered in detail in the next two chapters.

Conclusions

Staking has always been a contentious subject among those who bet on horses, but after the survey in this chapter it is possible to arrive at a set of conclusions which ought to settle matters, if not once and for all then at least in such a way that a lot of good wood is separated from the controversial trees.

1 Unless the backer's capital is unlimited and a bookmaker can be found to accept bets to any

amount, no staking plan can guarantee a profit before betting commences.

2 With the exception of the very risky, cover-to-win method which calls for unlimited resources, no staking plan can be constructed which will turn a big loss into a big profit.

3 Most staking plans will, at best, improve only marginally on level stakes.

4 Any staking plan can worsen the level-stakes position in the event of an unfavourable results pattern.

5 Plans which increase after losers may well not achieve their objective, and those calling for sharp increases in stakes can get the backer into deep water very quickly. Whatever the rate of increase, all plans of this kind involve chasing losses.

6 Increasing stakes after winners is recommended. Plans that increase the stakes gradually can do the backer little harm and may do some good. They are, it must be remembered, as much dependent on 'pattern' as any other sort of plan. When profits are boosted dramatically, careful managing is required if the backer is to emerge in a good position in the long term. Here the system operator can be likened to a financial investment manager who must decide when to take profits on the stocks and shares in which he deals.

7 Anyone using a staking plan of any type should avoid outsiders and even medium-priced selections which may produce long runs of losers.

3

Racing Permutations

Introduction

Properly adjusted staking on single selections is the safest way to restrict losses and enhance profits, but for the ordinary punter the relatively limited betting bank he/she has at his/her disposal means that any overall gain achieved will be correspondingly modest. An alternative to large stakes on singles is clever staking on cumulative wagers, based on doubles, trebles and accumulators, with which big wins are possible for only a small outlay. This approach obviously carries a greater element of risk, but speculative wagers of this sort can be constructed in such a way that steady profits may accrue even if a huge payout from a single coup eludes the backer. The use of racing perms, therefore, could in practice turn out to have a double vindication.

Popular Permutations

It is probably true to say that most racing enthusiasts have only a vague understanding of the complicated subject of permutation. Though perms are standard fare in Pools betting for instance, they are much less common in horse racing. In fact the limit of most punter's forays into the field is the following series of popular bets:

STANDARD PERMUTATIONS

Number of selections	Outlay in points	Name	Singles	Doubles	Trebles	Four-folds	Five-folds	Six-folds	Seven-folds
3	7	PATENT	3	3	1	—	—	—	—
4	11	YANKEE	—	6	4	1	—	—	—
5	26	CANADIAN or SUPER YANKEE	—	10	10	5	1	—	—
6	57	HEINZ	—	15	20	15	6	1	—
7	120	MULTI	—	21	35	35	21	7	1

The problem with these wagers, certainly the more ambitious of them, is that they only really pay off when all, or nearly all, of the punter's selections go in. Any reasonable win expectancy on the other hand results in a large wastage in stakes. For example, here is the position with the HEINZ bet when three winners are included:

WINNING BETS:
Doubles   3
Trebles   1

LOSING BETS:
Doubles   12
Trebles   19
Fourfolds   15
Fivefolds   6
Sixfold   1

Evidently prices would have to be very good indeed for punters even to recover their outlay, let alone start winning, on this rota of bets.

Reduction Plans – Doubles

With well-designed racing permutations, however, it is possible to go a long way towards cutting down on the damaging wastage of stakes.

Consider this simplest of examples:

Selections: A B C D
Two doubles: AC and BD

Thus, there are just two bets as against the usual six doubles on the four selections, yet there is a guarantee that three winners must produce a winning double. If either A or C are both successful, or B and D, the bet can win with less than the number of winners stipulated by the guarantee.

This type of arrangement is known as a reduction plan, and it can easily be extended to a greater number of selections by the simple rule of dividing the horses selected into two equal, or as equal as possible, groups and then backing each group with the number of doubles needed for full cover.

Here are plans for five, six and seven selections:

A
B   3 doubles
C
─────
D   1 double
E

Total: 4 doubles

Guarantee: one winning double if three winners are included among the five selections; three winning doubles if all in one section.

A
B   3 doubles
C
─────
D
E   3 doubles
F

Total: 6 doubles

Guarantee: at least one winning double if three winners are included in the six selections; three winning doubles if all in one section.

A
B   6 doubles
C
D
___
E
F   3 doubles
G

Total: 9 doubles

Guarantee: at least one winning double if three winners are included in the seven selections; three winning doubles if all in one section.

In these examples, prices need not be exceptional to recover outlay, provided the guarantee is met. In the last bet, three winners priced at no worse than 2–1 would automatically win back the total stake. Just two winners at that price would do the same should they fall together in either the top or bottom section of the wager, and better prices in either eventuality would naturally produce a profit, as would any number of winners over and above the minimum depending on how they are distributed among the nine possible doubles.

Reduction Plans – Trebles

It is easy enough to extend this idea to trebles, using the same basic formula of dividing the total number of selections into three groups as equal as possible, before covering for trebles from group to group in rotation:

A   Perm A and B with C or D
B   = 1 × 2 = 2 trebles
___
C   Perm C and D with E or F
D   = 1 × 2 = 2 trebles
___
E   Perm E and F with A or B
F   = 1 × 2 = 2 trebles

Total: 6 trebles

Guarantee: at least one winning treble, possibly more, if four winners are included in the six selections.

Also, regardless of the guarantee, punters would be justified in feeling slightly aggrieved if they backed three winners and the perm failed to line up a winning treble, although obviously this could happen.

To make sure that readers fully understand the principle involved with these bets, this is the formula for trebles stated in full:

1 Combine the number of possible doubles in the first group with each single selection in the second group.
2 Combine all the doubles in the second group with each selection in the third group.
3 Take the possible doubles in the third group with each selection in the first group.
4 If any group has three or more selections, stake on the actual number of trebles within it, in addition to the doubles.

These two examples illustrate the operation of the complete formula:

A	Perm two of A B and C with D or E
B	= 3 × 2 = 6 trebles
C	Perm D and E with F or G
D	= 1 × 2 = 2 trebles
E	Perm F and G with A B or C
F	= 1 × 3 = 3 trebles
G	Perm A B and C = 1 treble

Total: 12 trebles

Guarantee: at least one winning treble; possibly more if four winners are included in the seven selections.

And again:

A	Perm two of A B C and D with E F or G
B	= 6 × 3 = 18 trebles
C	Perm two of E F and G with H I or J
D	= 3 × 3 = 9 trebles
E	Perm two of H I and J with A B C or D
F	= 3 × 4 = 12 trebles
G	Perm three of A B C and D = 4 trebles
H	Perm E F and G = 1 treble
I	Perm H I and J = 1 treble
J	

Total: 45 trebles

Guarantee: at least one winning treble; possibly more if four winners are included in the ten selections.

When submitting bets of this sort to a bookmaker, they should be written out in the way shown below, giving the name of the selection first, followed by the letter, and adding on the appropriate instructions. Here is one for eight selections with the usual guarantee of a treble from four winners, and possibly only three.

THE BUTLER	A	Perm two of A B and C with D E or F
DEVON VICTORY	B	= 3 × 3 = 9 trebles
VENATE	C	Perm two of D E and F with G or H
OBERON	D	= 3 × 2 = 6 trebles
NO CATCH	E	Perm G and H with A B or C
ROSE OF DAMASCUS	F	= 1 × 3 = 3 trebles
DIAMOND GIRL	G	Perm A B and C = 1 treble
OFFICE BOY	H	Perm D E and F = 1 treble
		Total: 20 trebles

Recalling the earlier doubles formula, the same selections can be backed with a guarantee of one winning double from three successful nominations:

THE BUTLER	
DEVON VICTORY	6 doubles
VENATE	
OBERON	
NO CATCH	
ROSE OF DAMASCUS	6 doubles
DIAMOND GIRL	
OFFICE BOY	

Total: 12 doubles

Compound Perms and Accumulators

It is also possible to devise compound wagers which include accumulators as well as doubles and trebles. Here the aim is obviously a huge payout, with the doubles providing an element of insurance against things not going exactly according to plan. A series of such bets is set out below. They range from wagers with only limited aspirations, right up to the most ambitious assault on the bookmaker, but all give an excellent balance between cost and cover, and all have unshakeable guarantees. They are, therefore, much more than just hopeful gambles.

Five horses: A B C D E – 12 bets.
4 doubles: AD AE BC DE
3 trebles: ABD ABE CDE
5 fourfolds: ABCD ABCE ABDE ACDE BCDE

Minimum guarantees: three winners must give a double; four winners give two doubles, one treble and one fourfold.

Six horses: A B C D E F – 12 bets.
6 doubles: AC AF BD BE CF DE
6 trebles: ABE ACE ADF BCD BCF DEF

Minimum guarantees: three winners must give a double. Four winners must give one double and one treble.

Six horses: A B C D E F – 10 bets.
5 doubles: AB BC CD DE EF
4 trebles: ACE ACF ADE BDF
1 fourfold: ABEF

Minimum guarantees: Three winners must give either a double or a treble. Four winners give either three doubles, or two doubles and one treble, or two trebles, or two doubles. Five winners give four doubles and one treble, or three doubles, two trebles and one fourfold, or three doubles and three trebles.

Six horses: A B C D E F – 17 bets
6 doubles: AC AF BD BE CF DE
8 trebles: ACE ACF ADE ADF BCE BCF BDE BDF
3 fourfolds: ABCD ABEF CDEF

Minimum guarantees: Three winners must give a double. A winner in each of pairs A and B, C and D, E and F gives a treble. If two of these pairs all contain winners, there will be a fourfold.

Less patient backers may baulk at having to write out in full each component in the above wagers, but here is a plan which can be entered with little effort on just a few betting slips. It guarantees a massive pay out for an all-correct entry, with outstanding returns in the event of a near miss.

Seven horses: A B C D E F G – 77 bets.

7 Yankees (6 doubles, 4 trebles and a fourfold):

ABCF ABDE ACEG ADFG BCDG BEFG CDEF

Minimum guarantee: Five winners give the all-important fourfold which must produce a successful Yankee. Six winners give the cast-iron certainty of three winning Yankees. In both cases there will be outside doubles and trebles in support. Even with four winners, a Yankee is still possible and this number of correct forecasts, or even three or just two, will always give the punter some kind of consolation prize, the size of which will depend upon the prices and pattern of winners.

The principle of accumulated odds networking the same winners across the seven component Yankees makes this a real blockbuster of a bet, ideally suited to building up impressive gains, in particular from short-priced selections, where a high win-frequency is to be expected.

Another bet, less ambitious but equally effective in its way, again where the punter does not have to write out the names of his selections many times over, is set out below. Note that the horses must be numbered 1 to 6.

1	ROYAL DESIRE	Perm five consecutive doubles,
2	GRAND TOUR	four non-consecutive trebles, and
3	FAIR SHOW	numbers 1 2 3 4, numbers 1 2 5 6
4	LIMEVILLE	and numbers 3 4 5 6 in fourfolds
5	MACEDONIA	
6	RED PEAK	Total: 12 bets

A full check of all the wagers involved is as follows:

	Doubles				Trebles			Fourfolds	
1	X				X	X	X	X	X
2	X	X					X	X	X
3		X	X		X	X		X	X
4		X	X			X	X	X	X
5			X	X	X				X X
6				X	X	X	X		X X

This is a rather subtle arrangement in which three winners must yield a double and five winners a fourfold. Four correct guarantees either one double and one treble, or at the very worst a minimum of two doubles.

Finally, for those who prefer quantity rather than quality in their betting and like an interest in a large number of races, the pairs approach, though very risky, has the potential to win big if it clicks. The idea is to select a large number of horses in different races and to back them for fourfolds in the following manner:

12 selections

DOMESDAY
OUR CHARGER $\}$

DOMACILE
RELICARIO $\}$

SKATE IN
TONIN $\}$ Perm any two bracketed pairs

BEOTIEN
LEGAL ART $\}$ of selections from six pairs

WILD ROSE
BLUE MURDER $\}$ for fourfolds = 15 fourfolds

GRECIAN FLAG
ON APPROVAL $\}$

Here is a table which shows how many fourfolds are involved when a greater number of selections right up to 24 are covered in this way:

Selections	Pairs	Fourfolds
14	7	21
16	8	28
18	9	36
20	10	45
22	11	55
24	12	66

Winners *have* to fall together in pairs to count, and for this reason these are not the most professional of wagers, but they might appeal to someone who bets in very small amounts mostly for interest, but with the ever-present hope of a big win in the back of their mind. They are included here in what is a scientific treatise on racing as 'fun' bets, but they are offered without apology and in the knowledge that tastes vary in betting as much as in any other area of life.

Whatever readers take away from this chapter on permutation, it must now be clear that there is much more to betting than the tired old wagers pushed routinely over betting-shop counters by most punters every day. Racing perms take a wide range and, unlike most of the fancy bets promoted so aggressively by the bookmaking fraternity in their marketing and advertising, the best of them have very sound credentials as profit-makers.

4

Combination Bets

Introduction

Most backers, contemplating bets on doubles, trebles and accumulators, think in terms of only one selection per race. However, with the aid of some straightforward combination mathematics, it is perfectly feasible to enhance the probability of all-correct forecasts by covering two or more runners in opposition, in each of a series of events. Since, dead-heats apart, only one horse can win a race, this will always involve wasted stakes on losing animals. However, the principle governing cumulative bets whereby the odds of winners, plus one point, are multiplied together to arrive at the total return from a successful wager, means that the backer can be rewarded with a profit despite the inevitable loss of a part of the outlay.

Doubles

Take as an example the following bet which may easily produce acceptable gains on carefully selected non-handicaps where first and second favourites tend to monopolise results:

Race 1	
Race 2	24 doubles on
Race 3	first and second
Race 4	favourites

£24 staked

Provided races in which the first favourite is likely to start at odds-on are avoided, a good win is always on the cards from such a bet. Here is the full return from four winners at fairly short prices:

Race 1:   Second Favourite Won 11–4
Race 2:   Favourite Won 7–4
Race 3:   Favourite Won 2–1
Race 4:   Second Favourite Won 100–30

Double Races 1 and 2
Return: £1 × 3.75 × 2.75 = £10.31
Double Races 1 and 3
Return: £1 × 3.75 × 3.00 = £11.25
Double Races 1 and 4
Return: £1 × 3.75 × 4.33 = £16.24
Double Races 2 and 3
Return: £1 × 2.75 × 3.00 = £8.25
Double Races 2 and 4
Return: £1 × 2.75 × 4.33 = £11.91
Double Races 3 and 4
Return: £1 × 3.00 × 4.33 = £12.99

TOTAL RETURN: £70.95
OUTLAY: £24.00
NET PROFIT: £46.95

Thus, despite the luxury of backing two horses in each of four races, the bet has done very well indeed, measured by its return on outlay. Even three winners from eight nominations would always yield some sort of profit on any three of the prices shown, and just two would recover at least part of the total amount originally staked on the whole bet.

Combination bets of this type can be used on named horses as well as favourites. The backers' problem, apart from the very obvious and important one of locating sound selections for a wager, is to calculate the number of bets involved each time, assuming they wish to vary the number of horses in a race according to how they assess chances.

In the first place, however, it will help the reader's understanding if the 24 doubles in the foregoing illustration are written out in full:

Favourite (Race 1) with Favourite (Race 2)
Favourite (Race 1) with Favourite (Race 3)
Favourite (Race 1) with Favourite (Race 4)
Favourite (Race 1) with Second favourite (Race 2)
Favourite (Race 1) with Second favourite (Race 3)
Favourite (Race 1) with Second favourite (Race 4)
Second favourite (Race 1) with Favourite (Race 2)
Second favourite (Race 1) with Favourite (Race 3)
Second favourite (Race 1) with Favourite (Race 4)
Second favourite (Race 1) with Second favourite (Race 2)
Second favourite (Race 1) with Second favourite (Race 3)
Second favourite (Race 1) with Second favourite (Race 4)
Favourite (Race 2) with Favourite (Race 3)
Favourite (Race 2) with Favourite (Race 4)
Favourite (Race 2) with Second favourite (Race 3)
Favourite (Race 2) with Second favourite (Race 4)
Second favourite (Race 2) with Favourite (Race 3)
Second favourite (Race 2) with Favourite (Race 4)
Second favourite (Race 2) with Second favourite (Race 3)
Second favourite (Race 2) with Second favourite (Race 4)
Favourite (Race 3) with Favourite (Race 4)
Favourite (Race 3) with Second favourite (Race 4)
Second favourite (Race 3) with Favourite (Race 4)
Second favourite (Race 3) with Second favourite (Race 4)

In fact such long hand is unnecessary in practice. There is a simple formula which will calculate how many doubles are required for different numbers of horses in varying numbers of races. This is it:

Count the total number of selections. Multiply this number by one less than the total and divide by two. From the result deduct the aggregate of the possible two-selection combinations in each separate race.

Therefore in the doubles bet on the first and second favourites in four races, there were a total of eight selections. Multiply this by one less than eight to give $8 \times 7 = 56$, and divide by two $= 28$. In each of the four races there is one combination of two selections, that is the favourite with the second favourite, which cannot win. Deducting these four from 28 gives the correct total of 24 doubles needed to back the two betting-market leaders in the four chosen races.

Here is another example, this time for named selections and involving differing numbers of horses in only three legs:

Race 1:	SILVER DAY
	WELSH MOUNTAIN
	NETHERBY
Race 2:	SECURITY RISK
Race 3:	SELLY OAK
	SKI CHAMPION

Now there is a total of six selections. The formula provided gives the following number of doubles:

$$\frac{6 \times 5}{2} = 15$$

In Race 1 the three horses can be linked so as to give three combinations of two (Silver Day with Welsh Mountain, Silver Day with Netherby, Welsh Mountain with Netherby). Since only one horse is selected for Race 2, no combinations are possible there. In Race 3 Selly Oak and Ski Champion can be combined once. There are thus four combinations to be deducted from 15, producing a total of 11 doubles to be staked on.

The bet's instructions would be written as follows:

Cover for 11 £1 doubles
= £11 staked

When the winners of all three races are found, there will be three successful doubles, while two winners give one winning double. As always with combination bets, very short-priced selections must be avoided if a less than all-correct forecast is to show a profit or at least to recover a worthwhile part of the outlay.

If the above wager had had four selections in the first leg, rather than three, the total number of selections would become seven, giving

$$\frac{7 \times 6}{2} = 21$$

From this would be subtracted any two from four, that is six combinations in Race 1, none in Race 2 as before, and one in Race 3 again – seven ineffective combinations – yielding 14 doubles in all.

Trebles

Turning now to trebles, backing more than one horse in some or all of just three races presents few problems. All that is necessary to determine how many trebles must be staked on is to multiply together the number of selections in each event. For example:

Race 1:   CALL BOX
           SABLE SKIN
           KING'S DOWN

Race 2:   LADY JULIE

Race 3:   ALESSANDRO
           ANOTHER RONDO
           CANDY FLAKE

           One selection in each race
           = 3 × 1 × 3 = 9 £1 trebles
           = £9 staked

If King's Down at 4–1, Lady Julie at 6–4 and Candy Flake at 11–2 are the winners of the three races, the return will be 5 × 2.5 × 6.5 = 81.25, or £81.25 to a £1 stake, yielding a net profit of £72.25 on the £9 outlay.

When the strategy is applied to more than three races, however, the procedure to establish the total number of bets is slightly more complicated.

Take this rota of bets:

Race 1:   AFRICAN SLIPPER
           GRAND PRINCE

Race 2:   CAT'S WHISKER

Race 3:   CROUPIER
           BLUE LAGOON

Race 4:   COUNTRY CLUB
           CHYRIA
           SHAHID
           THE SQUIRE

The starting point for calculations is always to write out in full which trebles will be successful should one of the selections in each leg manage to win. Four races involve four trebles, five races 10 trebles, six races 20 trebles and seven races 35 trebles. In this case four races could produce these four winning trebles:

Races 1 2 and 3
Races 1 2 and 4
Races 1 3 and 4
Races 2 3 and 4

Now it is a simple matter to treat each combination of races as a separate entity, and to multiply the number of selections within it to arrive at the number of trebles, as with the earlier, three-race example:

Races 1 2 and 3 = $2 \times 1 \times 2 = 4$
Races 1 2 and 4 = $2 \times 1 \times 4 = 8$
Races 1 3 and 4 = $2 \times 2 \times 4 = 16$
Races 2 3 and 4 = $1 \times 2 \times 4 = 8$

Total: 36 trebles

Obviously four winners here would guarantee a profit, and three winners at reasonable odds (no worse than 2–1, 2–1 and 3–1 for instance) would recover outlay. Provided one gets the relationship between cover and total stake right, avoiding an excess of selections in too many legs, a wager like this enables one to cash in nicely when the reading of form narrows selected races down to just a few 'live' candidates in each.

Fourfolds

Calculations for fourfolds are exactly the same, where four races obviously make one fourfold, five races five fourfolds, six races 15 fourfolds, seven races 35 fourfolds. Here are a couple of examples:

Race 1:	SAN MARINO
	COME FORTH
Race 2:	FLAMING GLEN
	JUNGLE FOLLY
	IMPLICATED
	MAORI BOY
Race 3:	TOY SHOP
	SAVIC
Race 4:	TANGENT
	SOLID FUEL

One selection in each race
$= 2 \times 4 \times 2 \times 2$
$= 32$ fourfolds

Although 32 bets are involved here, only one of these can win. Winning horses at short prices (all around 11–8 for example) would do no more than recover outlay. But three such well-backed selections included with one at a starting price in the middle of the odds range would yield a really good gain. Even four winners at 2–1 would produce a return of $3 \times 3 \times 3 \times 3 = 81$ points, and a profit of 49 points.

This is an illustration of a bet for more races than the basic four:

Race 1:	BRIDGEOVER
	TOM BASKER
Race 2:	GAME VICTORY
	COURT WINGS
Race 3:	CHAMPOO
Race 4:	HORSE POWER
	STARS AND BARS
	QUIET MAN

Race 5:   WAR LEGEND
            NOW AND AGAIN

In this case, four from five races make five possible fourfolds and a grand total of bets calculated thus:

Races 1 2 3 and 4 = $2 \times 2 \times 1 \times 3 = 12$
Races 1 2 3 and 5 = $2 \times 2 \times 1 \times 2 = 8$
Races 1 2 4 and 5 = $2 \times 2 \times 3 \times 2 = 24$
Races 1 3 4 and 5 = $2 \times 1 \times 3 \times 2 = 12$
Races 2 3 4 and 5 = $2 \times 1 \times 3 \times 2 = 12$

Total: 68 fourfolds

This combination strategy need not be applied to doubles, trebles or fourfolds separately. A compound wager taking in two, or even all three, components, has lots of potential. A fairly inexpensive version might be:

Race 1:   CUBAN TAN
            WELSH JOKER

Race 2:   AVRO JET

Race 3:   RUM NEWS
            SET TO MUSIC

Race 4:   POET'S SON
            SILK TOWN

            Cover one selection in each
            race for 18 doubles, 20 trebles
            and 8 fourfolds

Combination Bets with Reduction Guarantees and Alternatives

Finally, before leaving combination betting, below is a wager of this type which also embraces the principle of reduction guarantees explained in the previous chapter. It allows the punter to cover three horses in each of four races, and reduces the cost of trebles from 108 to just 36 bets. The guarantee is that with four winners there must be at least one winning treble and an outside chance of four. At the same time it is only 2–1 against a winning treble if only three winners are found.

In making an actual bet each horse must first be assigned a letter depending on the race in which it is engaged. The sets of four trebles are then built up by transposition from the schedule.

Race 1: A B C
Race 2: D E F
Race 3: G H I
Race 4: J K L

AEIJ	4 trebles
AFGL	4 trebles
ADHK	4 trebles
BDFI	4 trebles
BDGJ	4 trebles
BEHL	4 trebles
CIKL	4 trebles
CEGK	4 trebles
CFHJ	4 trebles

Total: 36 trebles

Unfortunately the bet has to be written out on nine separate slips, for there is no way of expressing its structure clearly in one simple instruction. However, anyone who is prepared to take some trouble and give this method the chance it deserves could be well rewarded for their labours. With three horses in each race covered, some very big trebles indeed are possible when the selections at the more remunerative end of the odds scale actually win.

Combination bets as a whole are good value for the punter, therefore, but inevitably there will be those who are not comfortable with the wasted stakes that must be accepted as part and parcel of that approach to building up winning cumulative bets. Readers with such reservations might like to consider one final suggestion which still allows backers alternatives in the event of their main fancies being beaten.

Everyone will be familiar with the following tale of woe. You select two good candidates for a bet, but only one wins, while the other just fails. You have probably backed both of them to win, but the tasty double at cumulative odds has not materialised. At the same time you see to your chagrin that another horse, one over which you hesitated long and hard, comes home doing the proverbial handsprings. Perhaps another major fancy has won and run unbacked as well. After all, you cannot bet on everything you think will win.

The following pattern of bets could serve as the answer to this old, old story of 'what might have been', from which we must all have suffered at some time.

Two best bets, A and B, are chosen as before. They are still to be backed in a double, but two other horses with good chances in two more races are also selected. They can be called C and D. The final wager becomes:

> AB
> AC
> AD   Five doubles
> BC
> BD

Thus there are alternatives to each of the main fancies, but since all the selections are in different races, there is no wastage of stakes. All five doubles can win. Even if only the basic AB double comes up, reasonable prices will still produce a sound overall profit.

The same can be done with trebles. A and B are again the biggest fancies, but C, D and E are chosen as likely alternatives. Now the bet is:

ABC
ABD
ABE
ACD
ACE   Nine trebles
ADE
BCD
BCE
BDE

Thus if both of the main bets win, there are three additional selections which can make up at least one winning treble and possibly more. If one of them fails, all is not lost. Again there are horses in reserve. And once again the underlying principle of the whole bet is that each of the nine stakes can produce a win with no automatic loss of outlay.

Danger Selections

One final strategy for trebles is to include danger selections to the main fancy in each race rather than additional nominations in other races. Only one of the four trebles involved can win this time, but by using same-race alternatives you can give yourself excellent and cheap insurance against the annoying scenario of one loser in three that ruins so many ambitious trebles.

Here is the rota of bets:

	Selection	Danger
Race 1	A	D
Race 2	B	E
Race 3	C	F

Four trebles: ABC, ABF, ACE, BCD

Conclusions

This chapter as a whole offers a wide range of plans based specifically on the use of additional selections. If your natural betting inclination is not to put all your eggs in one basket, then there ought to be something in the foregoing pages to appeal to you. Combination bets are not the only way of playing safe at racing, but because big returns for a limited outlay are still possible with them, there is much to be said in their favour from both points of view.

5
Group Betting

Introduction

As was partly explained in Chapter 1 in the discussion on the concept of value, bookmakers bet to figures, and a knowledge of exactly how they do it is essential for backers, if only because it gives them a proper understanding of just what they are up against in the racing game. But professional gamblers bet to figures too. During their heyday between the World Wars, the legendary 'Old England', Charles Hannam and others successfully applied, in reverse, the bookmakers' own system of fixing the odds, and were able thereby to make a princely income from their betting activities.

Their method of making a 'book' against the 'book' on several horses in the same race which in their opinion held the best chances of winning nearly always involved betting at odds-on, and is not really for the ordinary backer who, unlike the professional, cannot operate in the racecourse Ring on a regular basis. Also, these men, along with their arch enemies, the top bookmakers, possessed a lightning facility with odds not given to ordinary mortals. Even so, within limits, the stay-at-home punter of only average mathematical ability can, on occasion, exploit their methods to good advantage.

Bookmakers' Percentages

The first step is to learn how a course bookmaker prices up his board on a race. Reading of form and racecourse 'intelligence' about stable confidence come into it, but the ruling principle in the structuring of a betting market is the price about each runner converted to a percentage. So a horse at Evens has a 50–50 chance of winning or 50 per cent, one at 6–4 a 60–40 chance or 40 per cent, a 3–1 shot is rated 75–25 or 25 per cent, and so on.

The method by which these percentage probabilities are calculated for all odds, including broken prices, is to add 1 point to the 'odds to 1' and divide into 100.

Example: 13–8 represents odds of 13 ÷ 8 = 1.625–1 plus 1 = 2.625; divided into 100 gives a percentage of 38.1, to one place of decimals.

This calculation can be done for every rate of odds to produce a table of percentages which may be consulted at a glance, thus obviating the necessity to do the maths every time.

RACING ODDS EXPRESSED AS A PERCENTAGE

Odds	%	Odds	%	Odds	%
8–15	65.2	9–4	30.8	12–1	7.7
4–7	63.6	95–40	29.6	13–1	7.1
8–13	61.9	5–2	28.6	14–1	6.7
4–6	60.0	11–4	26.7	15–1	6.3
8–11	57.9	3–1	25.0	16–1	5.9
4–5	55.6	100–30	23.1	18–1	5.3
5–6	54.6	7–2	22.2	20–1	4.8
10–11	52.4	4–1	20.0	22–1	4.3
20–21	51.2	9–2	18.2	25–1	3.8
Evens	50.0	5–1	16.7	28–1	3.4
21–20	48.8	11–2	15.4	30–1	3.2
11–10	47.6	6–1	14.3	33–1	2.9
6–5	45.5	13–2	13.3	35–1	2.8
5–4	44.4	7–1	12.5	40–1	2.4
11–8	42.1	15–2	11.8	50–1	2.0
6–4	40.0	8–1	11.1	66–1	1.5
13–8	38.1	17–2	10.5	100–1	1.0
7–4	36.4	9–1	10.0	150–1	0.7
15–8	34.8	19–2	9.5	200–1	0.5
2–1	33.3	10–1	9.1	250–1	0.4
85–40	32.0	11–1	8.3	500–1	0.2

The Bookmakers' Over-Round

Bookmakers know the numbers in this table like the back of their hand, and here is an example of how they would have used them to bet on a little race in the North of England:

Odds	Horse	%
11–10	LOXANDRA	47.6
11–4	MAMNOON	26.7
4–1	LAFTAH	20.0
8–1	SONGS OF INNOCENCE	11.1
25–1	TIAPHENA	3.8
40–1	EDINBURGH REAL ALE	2.4
50–1	CADEAUX PREMIERE	2.0
		113.6

In this case the 'over-round' on a 'round' book of 100 is 13.6 per cent. That is the bookmaker's 'edge' on the race and means that punters as a whole are always betting with him at that rate of disadvantage. The over-round varies from race to race depending on market conditions, but as long as the total of the odds about all the runners in a race converted to percentages exceeds 100, the bookmaker retains a favourable trading margin over his clients.

If, on the other hand, the aggregate of the percentages is less than 100, a punter could back every horse in the race and be certain of a profit. Suppose, for example, the above contest had been priced up as follows:

Odds	Horse	%
6–4	LOXANDRA	40.0
3–1	MAMNOON	25.0
9–1	LAFTAH	10.0
9–1	SONGS OF INNOCENCE	10.0
50–1	TIAPHENA	2.0

50–1	EDINBURGH REAL ALE	2.0
50–1	CADEAUX PREMIERE	2.0
		91.0

Now all an alert backer has to do is to stake according to the percentages to ensure a gain from the race whichever horse is successful:

Stake	Odds	Horse	Return
£40	6–4	LOXANDRA	£100
£25	3–1	MAMNOON	£100
£10	9–1	LAFTAH	£100
£10	9–1	SONGS OF INNOCENCE	£100
£2	50–1	TIAPHENA	£102
£2	50–1	EDINBURGH REAL ALE	£102
£2	50–1	CADEAUX PREMIERE	£102
£91			

The last three returns are not exactly to £100 because of the rounding of the percentages in the table up or down to one place after the decimal point, but it can be seen that for a total outlay of £91, the punter must make a profit of at least £9, whatever the result.

Improving the Backer's Percentages

No bookmaker would actually lay such prices and in the normal course of events when the 'book' is always over-round, the backer cannot 'steal' money in this way. You must always confront the percentage in excess of 100 which ensures that the overall odds on a race are in the bookmaker's favour, not yours. What you can do, however, is to take a view based on form as to which horses may win and which have only relatively poor chances, and then construct your own 'book' to give you the advantage if you are correct in your assessment.

Consider this example:

Odds	Horse	%
9–4	PROPHET MASTER	30.8
100–30	TOLANDRO	23.1
9–2	COLONISER	18.2
7–1	PETITE MARCHE	12.5
12–1	PANAWAY	7.7
12–1	WHY ELOPE	7.7
14–1	KIPSANG	6.7
14–1	SANDSHOES	6.7
20–1	GAY GORDON	4.8
33–1	CHINA TIGER	2.9
		121.1

Despite superficial appearances perhaps, this is not a particularly generous 'book' for punters with an 'over-round' of 21.1 per cent against them. If, for example, it is believed that the race can only go to one of the four market leaders, and the rest of the field has no real chance, then adding up the percentages, we get 30.8 + 23.1 + 18.2 + 12.5 = 84.6 per cent. This is the probability of one of these four winning, in the bookmaker's estimation. If a punter was to back them all in the manner illustrated above, this would mean betting at a rate of 15.4 per cent to 84.6 per cent, that is at odds of over 5–1 on. With six other horses in the field, clearly such a wager would be a very poor one because the risk is out of all proportion to the potential gain.

If the process of elimination is carried a stage further, it may be decided that the race lies between three, not four horses, namely Prophet Master, Coloniser or Petite Marche. Now the aggregate of the percentages is 30.8 + 18.2 + 12.5 = 61.5 per cent. That would mean betting at around 6–4 on. If a punter were supremely confident that analysis of the race was correct, this might well seem a reasonable bet. The bookmaker still holds the whip hand to the tune of 21.1 per cent over the totality of the punters betting on the race as a whole, but in terms of those particular fancies, the punter can take an acceptable profit on outlay and, like the bookmaker in relation to each individual client, can enjoy the luxury of having more than one horse on side.

At this point it is instructive to look at how a professional backer might approach this race. He/she is betting in the Ring and is in a position to exploit the competition for business between the various layers. Expert in reading the signs, the 'pro' steps in early when the favourite is on offer at 11–4. Coloniser is easy to back and although most bookmakers are offering 9–2, 11–2 is readily available with quite a few of them. When the favourite begins to shorten down to 9–4, Petite Marche, originally marked up at no better than 7–1, drifts to 10–1. Again having read the Ring signals correctly, the 'pro' once again gets the best of the odds and strikes the final bet on the race at that price. The percentage position about the three fancied animals is now:

Odds	Horse	%
11–4	PROPHET MASTER	26.7
11–2	COLONISER	15.4
10–1	PETITE MARCHE	9.1
		51.2

So the professional backer has improved the position by all of 10.3 percentage points, and for someone who makes their living at racing and habitually bets in large sums, this is a big difference. He/she now has just about even money to the three against the field and the chance of a very good profit.

Nevertheless, the professional can misread market trends too and, for the stay-at-home punter in the local betting shop, improving the margin in the above way may not seem all that significant. Nevertheless, properly applied in the right races, this professional method of group betting can be very effective even for the amateur speculator.

For example, the Derby at Epsom is an annual puzzle which most would be less than confident about solving with a single selection. The prices on a recent running for the fancied contenders were as follows:

11–4	REFUSE TO BEND
4–1	ALAMSHAR
9–2	BRIAN BORU
6–1	KRIS KIN
12–1	ALBERTO GIACOMETTI
16–1	NORSE DANCER
20–1	DUTCH GOLD
20–1	MAGISTRETTI
20–1	SHIELD
20–1	THE GREAT GATSBY
25–1	Bar

Suppose three horses were genuinely fancied – Alamshar, Kris Kin and Dutch Gold. The punter wishes to stake £15 on the race as a whole.

The first stage is the conversion of the odds available for each runner to a percentage probability, using the table given earlier:

Odds	Horse	%
4–1	ALAMSHAR	20.0
6–1	KRIS KIN	14.3
20–1	DUTCH GOLD	4.8

The aggregate of the percentages is 20.0 + 14.3 + 4.8 = 39.1 per cent. One needs to divide the intended £15 outlay by this figure to arrive at a basic betting unit:

$$£15 \div 39.1 = 0.384p$$
$$\text{Betting unit} = 38p$$

The stakes on each horse, therefore, will be:

ALAMSHAR	$20.0 \times 38p$ = £7.60	
KRIS KIN	$14.3 \times 38p$ = £5.43 or £5.40	
DUTCH GOLD	$4.8 \times 38p$ = £1.82 or £1.80	

Following this rota of stakes, the actual winner among the three selections will always produce approximately the same return and the same amount of profit:

Stake	Odds	Horse	Return
£7.60	4–1	ALAMSHAR	£38.00
£5.40	6–1	KRIS KIN	£37.80
£1.80	20–1	DUTCH GOLD	£37.80
£14.80			

Thus the punter is certain of an overall gain of about £23 if one of the three nominations wins, and in such an open race one might well be justified in considering this a better proposition than risking the whole of the £15 on just one candidate. The favourite, Refuse to Bend has been omitted because like most 2000 Guineas winners he is a probable non-stayer. Two of the next three horses in the market have been covered, and a likely outsider in Dutch Gold included in the bet. The punter has backed three excellent prospects for which £37.80 to £14.80 or odds of just over 5–2 against, has been obtained.

As we shall see in the next chapter, big handicaps, such as the Lincoln, the Royal Hunt Cup and the Cambridgeshire, offer little 'value' for the professional backer. Nevertheless, one can use the above formula effectively to back a lot of horses and still emerge with a sound gain.

Here is an example of how it could work on a recent renewal of one of the biggest betting races of the year, the Cesarewitch Handicap at Newmarket in mid-October. The fancied horses are:

12–1	LANDING LIGHT
14–1	DISTANT PROSPECT
20–1	DON FERNANDO
50–1	KRISTENSEN

Referring to the table, the percentages for each candidate are:

Odds	Horse	%
12–1	LANDING LIGHT	7.7
14–1	DISTANT PROSPECT	6.7
20–1	DON FERNANDO	4.8
50–1	KRISTENSEN	2.0
		21.2

Again the stake is to be £15, so that one betting unit will be £15 ÷ 21.2 = 71p. Multiply this by the percentage probability for every selection, and the final wager becomes:

LANDING LIGHT   7.7 × 71p = £5.47 or £5.50
DISTANT PROSPECT 6.7 × 71p = £4.76 or £4.70
DON FERNANDO   4.8 × 71p = £3.41 or £3.40
KRISTENSEN   2.0 × 71p = £1.42 or £1.40

The returns will be, given a winning selection:

Stake	Odds	Horse	Return
£5.50	12–1	LANDING LIGHT	£71.50
£4.70	14–1	DISTANT PROSPECT	£70.50
£3.40	20–1	DON FERNANDO	£71.40
£1.40	50–1	KRISTENSEN	£71.40
£15.00			

The rounding up or down of the percentages as shown in the table and of the stakes to the nearest 10p produces the slight difference in the rates of return but, should any horse win, there will always be a profit of around £56.

Obviously the wager can be extended to take in more horses in the race, provided some reduction in profit potential is accepted as the price to be paid for extra chances of finding the winner:

Odds	Horse	%
12–1	LANDING LIGHT	7.7
14–1	DISTANT PROSPECT	6.7
20–1	DON FERNANDO	4.8
20–1	RANDOM QUEST	4.8
25–1	ESTABLISHMENT	3.8
50–1	KRISTENSEN	2.0
		29.8

$$£15 \div 29.8 = 0.503$$
$$\text{Betting unit} = 50p$$

LANDING LIGHT $\quad$ 7.7 × 50p = £3.85 or £3.90
DISTANT PROSPECT 6.7 × 50p = £3.35 or £3.40
DON FERNANDO $\quad$ 4.8 × 50p = £2.40
RANDOM QUEST $\quad$ 4.8 × 50p = £2.40
ESTABLISHMENT $\quad$ 3.8 × 50p = £1.90
KRISTENSEN $\quad$ 2.0 × 50p = £1.00

Stake	Odds	Horse	Return
£3.90	12–1	LANDING LIGHT	£50.70
£3.40	14–1	DISTANT PROSPECT	£51.00
£2.40	20–1	DON FERNANDO	£50.40
£2.40	20–1	RANDOM QUEST	£50.40
£1.90	25–1	ESTABLISHMENT	£49.40
£1.00	50–1	KRISTENSEN	£51.00
£15.00			

Now six horses have been backed with a profit of around £35 guaranteed if any of the six wins. Someone playing the ante-post market just a few days before the race or, more safely, betting immediately after the overnight declaration has been announced, when wagers are on a 'non-runner, no bet' basis, could very probably improve this margin considerably by taking advantage of competitive prices that could well shorten up on the day of the event.

All in all, even if the average punter is not prepared to embrace group betting as a regular strategy, there will be times when it can prove very rewarding to careful racing fans who like to keep risks down to a minimum.

6
Selection Procedures

Introduction

Mathematical formulae and clever staking can only do so much. To win with any degree of consistency, punters must also find ways of regularly backing enough winners to allow the systematic arrangement of stakes to work in their favour. Over the years, many excellent methods of horse selection have been devised from many quarters, but no one has ever succeeded in finally laying down a set of rules which will automatically guarantee a profit from a given number of selections. If it were otherwise, the betting industry as we know it would have ceased to exist. On the other hand, by being ultra selective, procedures can be established which MAY, and here the emphasis is on the word 'may', indicate enough winning bets from a series to make an overall gain possible. However, this will most likely be only a percentage of the total outlay, with no absolute certainty of success.

This chapter offers no automatic selection systems with hard and fast rules which eliminate the need for punters to use their own judgement about which horses to back. Rather it presents a set of conclusions, based on statistics and experience, which in combination add up to a coherent strategy of selection. Racing has many facets, but seven main criteria are considered, and these are the ones which have the greatest bearing on results. Throughout, the object is to point readers firmly in the right direction when making decisions about the probable outcome of different sorts of races, while steering them away from the common mistakes which many punters habitually make.

Form – Race Ratings

Obviously the 'form' of racehorses must be the most important consideration in the process of selection. Definitions of form are legion but in general terms it can be said to be past running, particularly recent running, that is used as an indicator of probable future performance. This is a vast subject for study but even the most dedicated follower of the sport needs some relatively quick and easy way of assessing how one horse is likely to run in competition with others.

Fortunately nowadays, practically every sporting and national daily newspaper features race ratings, based on private handicaps compiled by journalists who specialise in the field. These are certainly the best measures of form which are readily available, but they must be used sensibly. They all have inherent weaknesses, not least the trap which a lot of inexperienced punters fall into of taking everything at its face value without reading between the lines.

This is where the other factors discussed in this chapter come in, although it is a fact that even by themselves, ratings, especially in non-handicap races, can be a very useful aid to winner-finding. In non-handicaps the weights to be carried are determined, not by the official handicapper intent on giving every runner an equal chance but, by the Weight-for-Age scale, usually with small, additional penalties for previous successes at various levels of competition.

Every horse has more or less the same chance, and the ratings given in numerical form in newspapers are a very fair assessment of what a horse has accomplished on the racecourse. Even so there is no guarantee that it will reproduce its known form and run exactly to the figure assigned to it by the compiler of the ratings. In non-handicaps generally the backer should obviously concentrate on the most highly rated horses, but without always expecting the top-rated horse of all to win. Just as important, they should avoid animals rated a long way behind those with the best figures.

The value of form-based race ratings in handicaps is much more questionable. If backers accept as the gospel truth the published numerical ratings, they are in fact doing no more than favouring the opinion of one expert over another, that is, the assessment of a private handicapper over the view of his official counterpart. The top-rated horse is the one which, in the opinion of the former, is best-in when the figures are compared with the weights actually allotted for a race.

Although newspaper ratings are certainly successful, some of the time, in pinpointing a horse which has been officially underestimated on current form, they still need to be treated with caution. As with conditions races, ratings in handicaps are more useful for indicating a small group from which the winner may come, rather than a single candidate apparently holding a decisive weight advantage on form. As a general rule they are most effective when a high rating, indicating a certain level of ability, is accompanied by evidence of very good recent running in similar company. Though it happens much less frequently than in non-handicaps, horses given no chance by the published figures can, and do, win handicap races.

But in the main, private handicaps in the form of race ratings, professionally compiled, provide an excellent quick guide to probable results. For all that, they are still only a guide. Punters who hope ultimately to be successful must definitely not rely on them alone. Because race ratings can never be the complete answer to their problem, they must be prepared to incorporate assessments derived from other factors into their overall view of likely performance.

Form Figures

Another form of assessment using a numerical approach is based on the study of form figures, that is the record of recent placings which in newspapers appear to the left of the name of each runner, where '1' indicates a win, '2' a second, '3' a third, '4' a fourth, and '0' or any other symbol an unplaced run, with the last-time-out figure given on the extreme right of the row. Many purists would no doubt argue that so simplistic an approach to the complex business of the study of form has little or no value, but the fact remains that many ordinary punters set great store by these figures.

Here two points need to be considered. First, do they in fact have a validity as an indicator of winners? Second, if so, which figures are of the greatest significance?

For the purposes of this book these two questions have been addressed via the medium of an extensive, statistical study, and a number of conclusions have been found to be inescapable and definitely proven.

The main finding was that horses having certain sets of form figures do consistently record more wins than others. Also, these superior figures, even when they fail to herald a win, produce a very high percentage of animals which reach a place.

In addition, three-figure form is much more reliable in both these instances than the now fashionable six-figure row carried by all newspapers in recent years. The reason for this is quite simple. Up-to-date form is always the best guide. Placings achieved four, five and six outings ago have less relevance to the present.

Finally, not only do certain form figures have undeniable value for the selector in non-handicap races – certainly in those where all the contestants have had a good few runs – the best of them also have considerable bearing on handicap events. This is true despite the fact that a run of good performances in races of this type, particularly one or more outright wins, will inevitably see a horse rise in the weights. The one exception to this finding is when a handicapper goes to the well once too often after recording a hat-trick of wins.

For several very good reasons, therefore, form figures may be regarded with considerable justification as a sound, shorthand summary of current racing ability and a good indicator of probable winners. However, those punters who already employ this approach tend to have widely differing views as to what are the best figures, and the reason for this is almost certainly that their preferences are not based on hard, statistical data.

Here this book fills an important gap, for below are listed those form figures, grouped into six ranks, which according to our comprehensive survey are most indicative of winners. It is also significant that they carry approximately equal weight in all types of race, not just when handicaps are compared with non-handicaps, but across the entire racing spectrum where gradations in the class of runners are extremely various. Also, even though the requirement to jump hurdles and fences in National Hunt racing cuts down the number of animals which actually record the sets of figures given below, they are as potent over the jumps as on the Flat in producing winners.

TOP RANK	111	(Not in handicaps)
	11	(Two career runs only)
SECOND RANK	101	
	131	
THIRD RANK	121	
	112	
FOURTH RANK	211	
	114	

FIFTH RANK   011

SIXTH RANK   311
                   321
                   122
                   21 (Two career runs only)

It is left to individuals to make the best use of this information in their own way but, combined with other recommendations in this chapter, judicious attention paid to the above rankings, if only as one selection factor among several, should assist in the quest for winners.

Betting Forecasts

The betting forecast is intended to give some indication of how the actual betting on a race is likely to go. Market moves can produce considerable variation from a newspaper forecast. Weight of money on the racecourse can alter the expected odds for individual horses quite dramatically, and also change the order in which runners are ranked by the ascending scale of available prices. More often than not, however, the forecasts provided via the press are remarkably accurate in predicting the make and shape of the final racecourse market on a race.

These betting forecasts are, in a very real sense, an assessment of the chances of at least the leading contenders for a given event, as indeed are the full range of odds offered by bookmakers at the track. The favourite is held to have the best prospects, the second favourite the next best, and so on for each runner whose relative chance is rated by its odds. Consequently there is at least a theoretical case to be made for using newspaper forecasts as an aid to selection, and practice confirms that punters can draw some positive conclusions from them, taking statistical evidence as their starting point.

Below is a complete breakdown for Flat, for National Hunt and for All-Weather Flat racing. The statistics show how the indications of the betting forecast fared over the entire British racing programme for a three-year period. The forecast used throughout was that of the leading racing daily.

FLAT – Turf

Stakes and conditions races (two-year-olds)
Favourite	38.2% won
Second favourite	22.5% won
Third favourite	13.6% won
Others	25.7% won

Stakes and conditions races (older horses)
Favourite	39.6% won
Second favourite	24.1% won
Third favourite	16.9% won
Others	19.4% won

Handicaps (all ages)
Favourite	24.6% won
Second favourite	18.3% won
Third favourite	15.2% won
Others	41.9% won

FLAT – All-Weather

Stakes and conditions races (all ages)
Favourite	38.1% won
Second favourite	22.7% won
Third favourite	20.9% won
Others	18.3% won

Handicaps (all ages)

Favourite	25.7% won
Second favourite	23.6% won
Third favourite	17.2% won
Others	33.5% won

NATIONAL HUNT

Non-handicap hurdles

Favourite	43.1% won
Second favourite	26.2% won
Third favourite	13.2% won
Others	17.5% won

Non-handicap chases

Favourite	42.4% won
Second favourite	25.1% won
Third favourite	12.6% won
Others	19.9% won

Handicap hurdles

Favourite	28.4% won
Second favourite	22.1% won
Third favourite	16.2% won
Others	33.3% won

Handicap chases

Favourite	37.6% won
Second favourite	22.9% won
Third favourite	13.1% won
Others	26.4% won

These figures are so impressive in a certain sense that no apology is offered for summarising them in a slightly different form:

FIRST THREE IN THE BETTING FORECAST

FLAT – Turf

Stakes and conditions races (two-year-olds)	74.3% won
Stakes and conditions races (older horses)	80.6% won
Handicaps (all ages)	58.1% won

FLAT – All-Weather

Stakes and conditions races (all ages)	81.7% won
Handicaps (all ages)	66.5% won

NATIONAL HUNT

Non-handicap hurdles	82.5% won
Non-handicap chases	80.1% won
Handicap hurdles	66.7% won
Handicap chases	73.6% won

These tables show that every type of non-handicap race under all three codes was dominated by the first three in the forecast. Even in handicaps, reputedly so much more difficult for the backer than conditions races, this group accounted for a significant proportion of the winners, although here there was quite a bit of variation between the three sorts of racing, Flat handicaps on grass showing the lowest percentage of all.

With this one exception, the impression left by all the above figures points to a single, overwhelming fact, namely that in most races *it is pointless to look beyond the first three in the betting forecast for the probable winner.* Punters may, on occasion, decide to depart from this rule, but if they do so, for whatever reason, they should be aware that they are flying in the face of a body of statistical evidence, the strength of which is quite unprecedented when it comes to betting on horses.

Backers aiming to find a single selection for a race would have to eliminate two of the three favoured quotes, but in terms of winning percentage alone, the significance of this factor in the search for winners can hardly be underestimated. Also, in acting on this conclusion, it is important to remember that the second and third quoted horses *taken together* often win more races than the first choice in the forecast. In other words, backers must not allow themselves to be mesmerised by a favourite for no other reason than that it happens to be the shortest price of the three horses with the best statistical chance.

Handicaps v. Non-handicaps

As we have already noted, in a handicap every horse is supposed to have the same chance. This equality is, however, only theoretical. Quite apart from any mistakes made by the Handicapper, current fitness and the vagaries of form ensure that in most handicaps the runners are strung out down the course just as in any other sort of race.

Also, weight affects different horses in different ways. A big horse is obviously more likely to be able to shrug off a sharp rise in its weight than a small one, and there are some racing experts who assert that weight 'off' has a different effect on running to identical weight 'on'. Again, a horse's reaction to fluctuations in the burdens it carries may be as much a matter of psychology as physical conformation.

All these factors are imponderables which are difficult, if not impossible, to measure accurately and tend to make winners much more difficult to spot in handicaps than in conditions races. On the other hand, because of their more open nature, prices for all runners including the favourite are generally better. This provides some justification for betting in races which are almost always harder to analyse.

Despite the complexities inherent in handicaps, it is

clear from the previous section that the first three in the betting forecast are still the most likely to succeed. These are the horses which, in the professional opinion of the compiler, have shown the best recent form, and results tend to confirm that this is a sound criterion for winner-finding, at least as a basic rule-of-thumb guide.

However, in handicaps rather than non-handicaps, another sort of horse is frequently given a prominent position in the actual racecourse market. This is the animal which has been performing indifferently in recent outings, but whose imminent return to form is heralded by much shorter odds than a literal interpretation of the Form Book would allow. Many of these horses win, particularly in Flat handicaps, and statistically account for a lot of winners which fall outside the favoured betting-forecast quotes. For punters picking out their selections well in advance of racing and indeed for anyone who bases their assessments on public form, such horses are an additional complication which add to the difficulties involved in betting on handicaps.

Trying to pinpoint horses which have been 'tuned up' to show a sudden, dramatic improvement in form after dropping significantly in the weights is one more handicap puzzle for the punter to solve. More will be said of this in the next section but, fitness aside, here are a number of simple guidelines. Used intelligently these should, at the very least, save those who chance their arm in handicaps a great deal of money in losing stakes:

1 Avoid handicaps with big fields. Realistically, unravelling a handicap of a maximum of about a dozen runners is the limit of anyone's ability as a form reader.

2 The fact that a horse was down the field last time out is no barrier to success in a handicap. Good recent form is still the best indicator but approach all handicaps

with an open mind. Look for and be prepared for the unexpected.

3   Sprints are much less reliable from a form point of view than races over a distance of ground. Sprint handicappers tend to beat one another with monotonous regularity, making a nonsense of the Form Book. Handicaps over a mile and a half or more, though relatively few in number, consistently see horses with good form near the top of the weights in the winner's enclosure.

4   Among trainers there is no such thing as a 'handicap specialist', despite an unfortunate tendency in the press to write up, in this way, any handler who has a purple patch. Trainers, like horses, have good runs and bad runs, and all trainers want to win handicaps. Except for an elite few, they are every stable's bread and butter. Some trainers on the other hand do make a speciality of winning handicaps on particular courses. Consistent success of this kind over a number of years is a matter of public record.

5   Never back a horse in a handicap ridden by an apprentice claiming the 7lb allowance. It is almost always an indication of lack of confidence on the part of connections when an inexperienced 'chalk' jockey is engaged to reduce the poundage to be carried by a highly weighted horse, even though there may be the occasional winning exception that proves the rule. Conversely, the booking of a top jockey by a small stable is a sure sign that a horse is 'expected'.

Each of the above negatives has a positive but, in the main, most bets should be made in non-handicaps. Even though prices may be lower, in the long run all punters stand or fall by a sound percentage of winners. Only bet in handicaps exceptionally when there seems a very good reason to do so. Even then, pre-race logic may well prove an expensive illusion in any race labelled a handicap.

Fitness

Away from professional racing circles, fitness in the thoroughbred racehorse is a much misunderstood concept. Amateur racing enthusiasts will certainly be helped in their appreciation of form if they have a proper insight into the business of preparing horses for the racecourse.

Initially they are readied for public performance by careful attention to feeding and diet, supported by slow and fast work to increase muscle power and tone. In the early weeks of a new season, when an animal has done few serious gallops at home, it may well carry an excess of 'condition', a racing euphemism for fat. Once it has been brought to a physical peak by regular exercise and a race or two, however, the overall state of its athletic well-being remains more or less constant for the rest of its active campaign. Occasionally, even when a horse's season is well advanced, it will 'blow' after a race, indicating that it has received only a very light preparation on the training grounds, and that it has been 'let down' after a period of intense activity. By and large though, most racehorses are near to peak physical fitness throughout the racing year. But, this is very far from being the whole story.

As a breed, thoroughbreds potentially have a large fund of nervous energy. That they are 'highly strung' is well known, and this nervous energy is the variable which, in the main, determines performance. If their energy reserves are low, they will not run as well as if their inner energy is at a high pitch. When an animal is galloped regularly, the nervous energy gradually builds up to a point where it can perform to its maximum capability on the racecourse. When it has been let down, on the other hand, it will have done only relatively easy home work, thus causing its reserves of nervous energy to decline, as well as producing some deterioration in physical tone.

Thus backers seeking to assess a horse's state of 'fitness' are immediately in difficulties, for they are not privy to stable secrets about the progress of inmates, and the evidence of the Form Book is frequently unhelpful, even confusing.

Horses hold their best form, made possible by a peak of physical fitness and nervous energy, for about a month. This period of racing 'mileage' can vary considerably, however. A horse which has been brought along very gradually will probably remain at a peak longer than one which has been given a rushed preparation. Even if it is assumed that every horse has undergone the best possible programme of training, the form cycle can vary significantly from the norm in certain animals. The problem for backers is that they, unlike the trainer, have no real knowledge of the individual characteristics of any horse they are interested in. Nor do they know what kind of preparation it has been given.

Hence it is very difficult for the independent assessor to chart with any degree of accuracy the progress of an animal's 'form wave', to use an old-fashioned expression. A horse wins a couple of races in quick succession for example, then goes out like a light when heavily backed next time it runs. How could the form student have known that the horse was stale, with its reserves of nervous energy temporarily depleted? The answer may well be that not even the trainer was able to assess accurately the fine line between their charge being at its peak or just 'over the top'.

Just to take one example from the very top level of Flat racing, not from the lower echelons where inconsistent form is axiomatic. Rakti looked a champion racehorse of the very highest class when he followed up his win in the Champion Stakes of the previous season with a stunning success first time out in the 2004 season in the Prince of Wales's Stakes at Royal Ascot. As a result, trainer Michael Jarvis's magnificent specimen of a five-year-old entire looked unbeatable on form in the Eclipse Stakes over the same distance 17 days later. In that race Rakti started a hot favourite but, perfectly placed to win in the straight, dropped away tamely once the sprint for the line began and finished a well-beaten eighth. The horse had 'bounced', to use a racing expression, and evidently his tremendous victory at Ascot had taken far more out of him than his trainer, let alone anyone else, realised.

Conversely, what about the huge number of animals which are repeatedly run when short of the gallop that brings them to their peak until their trainers are satisfied that they can win off their current handicap mark? How can the backer divine when the horse is finally 100 per cent fit? Also, can even the cleverest trainers ever be certain that their timing is exactly right?

Horses are not machines, and gambling trainers, as well as punters, and even the handlers of horses due to run in a Classic race, must accept the fact. However, there is a simple test that students of form can apply and though it cannot help them to form definite conclusions about the beginning and end of the 'form wave', it will provide a reasonable indication of whether a horse is likely to reproduce good recent form.

Below are the results of a survey covering 500 races on the Flat and 500 for National Hunt racing taken at a time when the season in question was in full swing. It classifies each set of 500 winners according to how many days had elapsed since their immediately previous public outing:

FLAT – 500 races

Winners running within:

1–7 days	17.7%
8–14 days	26.3%
15–21 days	21.1%
22–28 days	21.4%
29+ days	13.5%

NATIONAL HUNT – 500 races

Winners running within:

1–7 days	18.8%
8–14 days	28.1%
15–21 days	26.4%
22–28 days	16.8%
29+ days	9.9%

Since 86.5 per cent of the Flat races were won by horses reappearing within 28 days of their previous run, it is possible to formulate a '28-day-rule' – no horse should be backed if more than 28 days have elapsed since its last racecourse appearance. To make this into an absolute rule might be going too far, but certainly any horse that has been off the track for more than about a month must be treated with the greatest caution.

Similarly for National Hunt racing, a 28-day rule could also be applied, but in this branch of the sport where fitness is vital over the longer distances involved and because of the necessity to jump obstacles, it is worth noting that a '21-day rule' would have yielded no fewer than 73.3 per cent of the jump winners in the survey.

These considerations are a positive aid to finding winners. The only type of race in which they are of very little value, as a matter of course, are Group 1 and 2 contests involving the cream of the horses of each generation. With these animals the four-week 'form wave' does not apply, at least in so far as public performances are concerned. Aimed for just a few top races each season, the best horses are delivered to the racecourse to compete in the Classics and the like at a peak of physical and nervous fitness every time, or at least that is what their trainers hope and believe. They know that all horses have a low 'mileage' and bring their best animals to a peak at home, thus avoiding too many exhausting contests at the highest level on the racecourse.

Trainer Form

In the last few years there has been an explosion of statistics of every kind about racing available to the enthusiast who is keen to study the sport in depth. It is now realised that in many ways human beings are a more reliable factor than horses. Unlike the performance of thoroughbreds, which can vary greatly from race to race, and often for no apparent reason, the men and women responsible for their preparation and placing in races are in the main highly consistent in their methods. Hence, the modern preoccupation with trainers' records which, in the case of certain experts, amounts to an alternative that transcends the conventional assessment of form as a way of picking out which horses to back. This section stops a long way short of embracing such a radical approach but there can be no doubt that the punter can draw many valuable lessons from an intimate knowledge of 'trainer form'.

Under all codes of racing, Flat and jumps, there are many trainers, but season after season a small group of handlers regularly do much better than the rest. This is due, above all, to their skill at their chosen profession which attracts to their yards the best horses from the most committed owners with the financial means to breed, or to buy from the available pool of bloodstock, those animals most likely to succeed on the racecourse.

In a recent Flat season for example, the top 12 trainers in the numerical winning list sent out between them no fewer than 994 winners. This comes to about one-fifth of the races run in Britain during that period. Similarly over the jumps the top 12 stables accounted for no less than 958 winners in a single National Hunt season. There are slightly less jump than Flat races during a season, and there are many more trainers operating under winter rules, including the large army of permit holders. Therefore, 958 winners is a very impressive record of achievement for just a small group of yards.

Winning percentages vary from over 25 to under 15, but what is important here is the sheer volume of successes notched up by the top echelon of the training establishment. Leaving aside the form of the horses themselves, it must make sense for the backer to concentrate on the charges of the leading trainers, for they will always have a head start, statistically, over runners from other stables. There may be occasions when there are grounds for looking beyond the small training elite, but as a general approach there is a lot to be said for mentally upgrading the chance of any horse trained by one of the most successful handlers in terms of wins, the more so as the percentage strike rate of their rivals is no better and in most cases a great deal worse than theirs.

This is particularly true in Flat non-handicaps. In this area the top yards are able to achieve their huge haul of winners year after year because they have a virtual monopoly of the better-class horses which can be exploited in stakes and conditions races. In handicaps the equalisation of chances by weight has the effect of neutralising their position. In any race that is not a handicap, trainers of the calibre of Mick Channon, John Gosden, Barry Hills, Richard Hannon, Mark Johnston, Sir Michael Stoute and several others have a priceless advantage, and backers who ignore the fact do so at their peril.

Effect of the Draw

In some races on some courses the effect of the draw cannot be exaggerated. The results of certain sprints, and even of contests up to a mile in distance, can be greatly influenced by a good draw, with those badly drawn having virtually no chance.

On the other hand, it would be wrong to make too much of this factor at many venues where the starting positions of runners only marginally influence results, and in some cases not at all. Also, ground conditions and the position of the stalls can often play havoc with preconceived notions about what constitutes a favourable draw.

Below is a short list of courses and distances where this factor in the circumstances given always has a vital role to play. In every case, big fields obviously magnify the advantage to a well-drawn animal.

Draw Advantage

High

Beverley:	5f–8f, except on very heavy ground.
Folkestone:	6f–7f, on any ground, but especially on soft.
Goodwood:	7f–8f, on good or faster ground.
Hamilton:	5f–8f, on any ground, but especially on soft.
Redcar:	5f–8f, especially on soft ground.
Salisbury:	5f–8f, on fast ground only.
Sandown:	5f, on any ground, but especially on soft.
Thirsk:	5f–6f, except on soft or heavy ground.
Windsor:	5f–6f, but only on good or faster ground.

Low

Chester:	Up to 8f, on any ground, given a fast break.
Lingfield Park (All-Weather):	
	5f–8f on standard going.
Pontefract:	5f–8f, except on very heavy ground.
York:	5f–8f, on any ground, but especially on soft.

In addition, on certain courses the draw can be absolutely crucial in deciding the outcome of races, but this can vary from season to season, usually due to ground conditions. Races with big fields on the straight courses at Ayr, Doncaster and Goodwood in particular fall into this category. Here the backer is recommended to study the bias as the meeting develops before drawing any definite conclusions about a decisive, prevailing trend.

For as long as organised racing and betting have taken place, indeed long before that, horses in competition have regularly made fools of us. A racehorse is not a robot and will not always do what is expected of it. Nevertheless, form allied to a strong dash of commonsense is still the punter's best means of attack and defence in the battle with the bookmaker. Experience and flair come into it too, but it is hoped that this chapter will have provided some immediate insights that would otherwise have taken many years to acquire through trial and error. And perhaps, not even then!

7
Racing Systems

A System for the English Classics

In the early 1960s a number of racing scribes, writing in several different publications, began to call attention to what was heralded as 'the system that always wins' or, put another way, 'the system that never loses'. It seems that they had stumbled on the fact that every year for a century or more, with just a very occasional exception, at least one favourite had won an English Classic in the course of a season. However limited in scope, here was a system to 'beat the book'. A staking plan was attached and the idea enthusiastically written up as a goldmine for punters.

Double up on Classic favourites every year, so the argument went, and a profit was always there for the taking. True enough of course, except that an odds-on chance at the wrong place in the sequence can still produce a loss, even if the condition of one winning favourite per year is fulfilled.

Since then, tradition being the ruling canon of English racing, things have gone on pretty much as before, and only very, very rarely has the minimum standard of one winning Classic favourite out of five not been met.

Readers might well object that up to five bets a year and a single winner – for clearly there can be no more bets after one win in the sequence has been recorded – add up to a swallow which is hardly likely to make a racing fan's summer. Even so, a detailed examination of the idea will serve very well as an introduction to this chapter on automatic racing systems, that is, betting procedures which generate selections from a set of strict rules and which call for no judgement, or very little, on the part of the operator.

Here is the complete record of favourites in the English Classics in the last 10 years. Year 10 in the table represents the most recent renewal of the annual series of races.

**RECORD OF CLASSIC FAVOURITES
OVER A 10-YEAR PERIOD**

	2000 Guineas (Newmarket, May)	1000 Guineas (Newmarket, May)	Oaks (Epsom, June)	Derby (Epsom, June)	St Leger (Doncaster, September)
Year 10	Lost	Lost	Lost	Lost	Won 5–4
Year 9	Lost	Lost	Won 100–30	Lost	Lost
Year 8	Lost	Lost	Won 3–1	Won 11–4 jt	Won 13–8
Year 7	Lost	Lost	Won 9–4	Lost	Won 11–4
Year 6	Lost	Won 4–1	Lost	Lost	Lost
Year 5	Lost	Won 100–30 jt	Lost	Lost	Won 5–2
Year 4	Lost	Lost	Won 5–6	Lost	Won 5–4
Year 3	Lost	Won 10–11	Lost	Lost	Lost
Year 2	Lost	Lost	Lost	Lost	Won 100–30
Year 1	Lost	Lost	Lost	Won 7–2	Lost

There can be no doubt that the incidence of winning Classic favourites has declined in recent years. Whereas up to the 1980s and early 1990s the strike rate was running at around 50 per cent, now the figure has dropped to as low as 30 per cent. This may not be a permanent trend but, even so, the table shows quite clearly that the idea behind 'the system that always wins' still has the potential to turn up a profit with a regularity which is highly unusual in the risky business of backing horses.

To give some indication of the profit potential of the plan in monetary terms, on the next page is the financial record to an opening stake of £10 for the last five years, by which time the new order of running the Classics occasioned by changes to the annual fixture list in the 90s had become permanent.

The recommended method works on a pre-planned rota of bets as follows:

2000 Guineas	£10 Win	FAVOURITE (unnamed)
1000 Guineas	£20 Win	FAVOURITE (unnamed)
Oaks	£40 Win	FAVOURITE (unnamed)
Derby	£80 Win	FAVOURITE (unnamed)
St Leger	£160 Win	FAVOURITE (unnamed)

FINANCIAL PERFORMANCE OF BETTING ON CLASSIC FAVOURITES OVER A FIVE-YEAR PERIOD

Year 6

2000 Guineas	Lost	–£10.00
1000 Guineas	Won 4–1	+£80.00
	Profit	+£70.00

Year 7

2000 Guineas	Lost	–£10.00
1000 Guineas	Lost	–£20.00
Oaks	Won 9–4	+£90.00
	Profit	+£60.00

Year 8

2000 Guineas	Lost	–£10.00
1000 Guineas	Lost	–£20.00
Oaks	Won 3–1	+£120.00
	Profit	+£90.00

Year 9

2000 Guineas	Lost	–£10.00
1000 Guineas	Lost	–£20.00
Oaks	Won 100–30	+£133.33
	Profit	+£103.33

	Year 10	
2000 Guineas	Lost	–£10.00
1000 Guineas	Lost	–£20.00
Oaks	Lost	–£40.00
Derby	Lost	–£80.00
St Leger	Won 5–4	+£200.00
	Profit	+£50.00

Despite the variability in outlay and returns, as a result of where winners fall in the sequence and their starting prices, the system produced the expected profit each year. Nothing here to guarantee a life of comfort for the rest of your days, but 'a profit is a profit' as every racing fan and stockbroker will tell you.

The Sprint Championship and the Cup Races

There are a couple of other natural big-race series in the Flat Calendar which lend themselves to the application of the idea, namely the Sprint Championship made up of the leading five Group races in the season over the minimum five-furlong trip, and the five Cup races for stayers. Let us see what happens when the Classic system is extended to them.

Overleaf is a table which shows the record of favourites in the top sprint races in the last five years. The most recent season is represented by the column on the right, that is Year 5.

PERFORMANCE OF FAVOURITES IN THE SPRINT CHAMPIONSHIP OVER A FIVE-YEAR PERIOD

Sprint	Year 1	Year 2	Year 3	Year 4	Year 5
Palace House Stakes (Newmarket, May)	Lost	Lost	Lost	Won 2–1	Won 9–4
Temple Stakes (Sandown, May)	Lost	Lost	Won 100–30 jt	Lost	Won 5–2 jt
King's Stand Stakes (Royal Ascot, June)	Lost	Lost	Lost	Lost	Lost
King George Stakes (Goodwood, July)	Won 6–1	Lost	Lost	Lost	Won 11–4
Nunthorpe Stakes (York, August)	Won Evens	Won 5–2	Won 4–9	Won 3–1	Won 4–9

Therefore the £10 – £20 – £40 – £80 – £160 sequence with a stop-at-a-winner provision would have yielded a profit every year, just like the Classics in the same period.

However, when the results for the sequence of Cup races in the five seasons under review is examined, it has to be admitted that a less rosy picture emerges.

PERFORMANCE OF FAVOURITES IN CUP RACES OVER A FIVE-YEAR PERIOD

Cup Race	Year 1	Year 2	Year 3	Year 4	Year 5
Yorkshire Cup (York, May)	Lost	Won 15–8	Lost	Won 2–1	Lost
Gold Cup (Royal Ascot, June)	Lost	Won 11–8	Lost	Lost	Lost
Goodwood Cup (Goodwood, July)	Won 9–4 jt	Lost	Lost	Lost	Lost
Doncaster Cup (Doncaster, September)	Lost	Lost	Lost	Lost	Lost
Jockey Club Cup (Newmarket, October)	Lost	Lost	Lost	Lost	Lost

It can be seen, therefore, that there were complete failures in two years out of five and quite a substantial loss would have resulted from using the recommended staking plan in those years. There are two points to make here. First, races for top-class stayers are few and far between in the Racing Calendar, and form is not sufficiently exposed to make the favourite as sound a proposition as in the Classic and sprint sequences where the market has much more form to work on in order to arrive at a good favourite. Second, and arguably more important, the Cup sequences demonstrate that however good a system might be much of the time, it will always be impossible to remove the gamble inherent in every bet or every series of bets on horses.

That said, surely enough statistics have been cited to convince readers that wagers on a series of five non-handicaps in the way recommended have a great deal of profit potential, even allowing for the occasional complete failure.

In the remainder of the Group 1, Group 2 and Group 3 programmes on the Flat there are no natural sequences like the above, although similar winning percentages for favourites can be expected overall. Some readers might like to try their hand at dividing the Group programme into sets of five, and betting in the recommended manner on each separate, predetermined sequence.

Another alternative might be to pick out in advance from the weekly racing programme five-race sequences of non-handicaps which, statistically, have an excellent record for favourites. Saturday would be the best day for such an approach – on other days there would seldom be enough meetings with suitable races on which to operate. Staking down the series in chronological order in a betting shop or by telephone should lead most of the time to some sort of profit.

Some people say that racing systems are bunk. It is the

belief of the present writer that the foregoing few pages, and in particular the Classic method, 'the system that never loses', prove beyond all doubt that methodical betting using a clear set of predetermined rules is anything but, provided that the principles on which it is based are sound and have a foundation in the statistical record to suggest that profits are likely to accrue. The rest of this chapter contains examples of successful betting that likewise bear out this contention.

How to Pick the Derby Winner

In the far-off days of the great owner-breeder aristocrats who once dominated the English Turf, the pinnacle of human achievement in the equine field (and, for some of them, in *any* field) was to breed the winner of the Epsom Derby. Nowadays, the heirs of that almost defunct species are more concerned with shoring up the decaying stately pile; and although commercial breeding operations still keep a weather eye on the greatest prize in racing, such is the tremendously wide, international – not to say global – nature of the sport, that the odds against a single individual or organisation actually attaining the dream are of National Lottery proportions.

It is true, however, that for the common or garden British punter, to try to back the Derby winner is even now the racing conundrum that annually offers the greatest challenge and, if successful, the greatest sense of self-satisfaction, irrespective of financial reward. The Prix de l'Arc de Triomphe and the Breeders' Cup series of races in America may outrank the Derby in prize money, but in terms of prestige and sheer interest the big race on Epsom Downs in June is still a national event that transcends the sport which gave rise to it. Everyone, without exception, from the highest to the lowest in the land, wants to pick the Derby winner.

In fact, most Epsom Derby winners match a distinct

profile and, if you know what the profile is, finding this year's or any year's winner is not so daunting a task as most people usually find it.

Without further ado, therefore, here are the principal elements of the profile:

1 The Derby winner will usually come from the first six in the betting. If two or more horses are quoted as sixth equal in the betting, or different bookmakers have two different horses in sixth place, it would be permissible to include a seventh or even an eighth horse in calculations. By and large, however, this 'rule of six' invariably pinpoints horses that can win a modern renewal of the big race.

2 The Derby winner will usually have one of the following sets of three-figure form to its name:

111	121	011
11 $\rbrace$(two career	112	311
21 $\,$runs)	211	321
101	114	122
131		

This may seem too simplistic for the sophisticated racing enthusiast accustomed to thinking in terms of lengths and pounds as a means of comparing the past performances of racehorses, but the fact remains that no less than 10 of the last 12 Derby winners at the time of writing fulfilled this deceptively straightforward qualification.

Applying these two rules will generally reduce the Derby field to two, three or perhaps four live candidates. The secret of making a final, single selection that is likely to be correct is to examine two-year-old form, which is much more important for the Derby than most people realise.

The following guidelines are drawn from years of

statistics for the big race, and although no one guide will pinpoint the winner every year, intelligent inference may point the clever punter in exactly the right direction much of the time.

1   Thirty-six of the last 41 Derby winners won at seven furlongs or a mile as two-year-olds.

2   Derby winners are hardly ever beaten at two after winning their maiden race, unless in a Group or Listed event.

3   Excluding Group or Listed races, most Derby winners attracted favourable Form Book comments in their last two-year-old race in non-Pattern company. Won 'easily', 'comfortably', 'readily', 'leading all the way' or 'soon clear' from one or two furlongs out, or 'impressive' are the type of comments to look for.

4   If they ran before the first week in August at two, most Derby winners have subsequently been placed in the first four in a Group race before their juvenile career ends.

5   If they made their racecourse debut after June, quite a number of Derby winners had their first run, successful or not, on either of the straight courses at Newmarket (July Course or Rowley Mile) or on the straight course at Newbury. Kris Kin, the 2003 winner, is the most recent example of this factor.

The author has backed a number of recent Derby winners using this profile. To cite past, personal successes would probably cut little ice with readers, however, for the proof of the pudding is always in the eating.

However, space does permit at least one illustration of the formula in action, and the race for the most recent Derby at the time of writing will do very well to demonstrate how effective its simple precepts can be.

Here were the first six in the betting according to the prices advertised by one of the 'Big Three' bookmakers in the morning newspapers on the day of the race.

5–2	NORTH LIGHT
5–2	SNOW RIDGE
7–1	SALFORD CITY
15–2	PERCUSSIONIST
8–1	AMERICAN POST
14–1	PUKKA

Let The Lion Roar and Rule of Law, both quoted at 16–1, were just outside the first six in the market and, strictly speaking, were candidates for immediate elimination. A look at their form figures, however, confirmed that they should not be considered. Let The Lion Roar had 2–13 before its name, and the three-figure form of Rule of Law was 13–2. Neither set of figures match those given in Rule 2 of the formula, and it was possible to proceed to the actual first six in the betting without any further qualms. The form figures for those six horses were as follows:

21–1	NORTH LIGHT
10–2	SNOW RIDGE
1–10	SALFORD CITY
2–11	PERCUSSIONIST
–111	AMERICAN POST
31–1	PUKKA

Two horses, Snow Ridge and Salford City lacked the essential level of form revealed by the tell-tale form figures of Rule 2. They could be struck off the list without further ado.

That left four horses, and now it was necessary to

analyse each from the more difficult angle of their two-year-old record. It is just before this stage that most people's examination of form would stop, but the value of looking very closely at how the horses ran as juveniles is amply demonstrated by the analysis set out below.

NORTH LIGHT. This colt made its debut at Sandown in August but did not win until contesting its second maiden, this time at Goodwood over a mile, where it won by 1¾ lengths, having been 'pushed clear inside the final furlong', winning 'readily'. It did not run again as a two-year-old.

Its debut comparatively late in the season exonerated it from attempting races of Pattern class, and although it had not made its first appearance over the easy straight courses at either Newbury or Newmarket, usually favoured by most Classic trainers for an introductory run, the rest of its juvenile record matched the formula's profile for a horse's two-year-old career well enough. North Light had to be considered as a horse with a real chance of winning the big race at three.

PERCUSSIONIST. This candidate had failed the most important two-year-old test of all – it had not won over at least seven furlongs at two. In fact it was beaten in both of its two-year-old races, each of them for maidens. This was hardly the profile of a future Derby winner. The formula allowed a very confident elimination.

AMERICAN POST. The French-trained runner had won the Racing Post Trophy over a mile at Doncaster at two. Apart from its first two outings in small races in France, the second of which it had won by two lengths, after being 'pushed out', American Post had run in nothing but Listed or Group races for the rest of its juvenile campaign, winning on each occasion. Clearly its form at two made it an obvious candidate for inclusion in any short list.

PUKKA. As a two-year-old, Pukka had contested a number of maiden races before finally winning the fourth of them on the all-weather track at Lingfield Park over 10 furlongs in November. It was reported by the Form Book as 'soon in command, pushed out'. The colt did not appear again at two. This was far from being the form of a typical Derby winner but, following the formula to the letter, it could not be faulted, even though its record was definitely lacking most of the factors which are considered desirable in the two-year-old record. Pukka would have been included in the final analysis of the race for the Derby.

Thus the three stages of analysis laid down by the formula gave just three horses to consider as the possible winner of that year's big race: North Light, American Post and Pukka.

After that it would have been up to the individual to decide. North Light won at 7–2, American Post failed to stay, and the gambled-on Pukka finished down the field, as might have been expected of a horse which had never run in anything better than handicap company. This was by no means a perfect result for the formula, but as usual the eventual winner of the race had been included in the final short list indicated by it.

That was the past. In the future, readers will be able to see for themselves how well the formula does as each renewal of the Derby comes around, but there is every reason to believe that it will not be very wide of the mark most years in highlighting the winner from a very small group of possibles.

Royal Ascot Handicappers

Royal Ascot is without doubt the most competitive meeting of the year in Britain, for Flat racing at least. Finding winners there has always been very difficult but, precisely because of its competitiveness, the June festival can be the source of future winners, provided the form-minded punter looks in the right place. For although form in the top-class non-handicaps is not always upheld in later races, the hotly contested handicaps can give positive clues about possible winners in the weeks that follow the meeting.

As we shall see later in this chapter, horses with the higher weights in handicaps have the best chance. Class tells, and weight below the saddle has only so much stopping power against inferior rivals. The same applies when looking at a handicap with a view to picking out from it those animals likely to win in near-at-hand engagements. Horses that ran well at Ascot with a big weight are the ones most likely to come out and convert their good showing into an actual win in handicaps which, in most cases, will not be quite the class of their Royal Ascot event.

The basic system rules are therefore very simple:

1   In all handicaps run during the five days of Royal Ascot, list those horses which occupied the second down to the sixth place and were carrying 9 stone or more.

2   Qualifiers are given two chances to win, in either handicaps or non-handicaps, excluding races abroad.

3   Stop betting on a listed horse after a win.

Starting on the next page are the results for this straight-forward betting strategy in three recent seasons, where the results headed 'Year 3' are from the most recent season.

RUNNERS IN ROYAL ASCOT HANDICAPS
SECOND TO SIXTH, CARRYING 9 STONE OR MORE
TWO CHANCES TO WIN; STOP AT A WIN

Year 1

Duke of Edinburgh Stakes

AKBAR (5–9–11)	Won 5–4
GALLERY GOD (5–9–5)	Lost, Lost
HATHA ANNA (4–10–0)	Won 1–3
MUTAKARRIM (4–9–1)	Lost
SOLO FLIGHT (4–9–1)	Lost, Lost

Royal Hunt Cup

BLUE MOUNTAIN (4–9–4)	Lost, Lost

Ascot Stakes

FIRST BALLOT (5–10–0)	Lost, Won 5–1
MANA D'ARGENT (4–9–0)	Lost, Lost

King George V Stakes

TOMASINO (3–9–2)	Lost
REGATTA POINT (3–9–3)	Lost, Lost

Britannia Stakes

ECCLESIASTICAL (3–9–0)	Did not race

Wokingham Stakes

INDIAN SPARK (7–9–4)	Won 7–2
DOCTOR SPIN (5–9–6)	Lost, Lost

Fern Hill Rated Stakes

DEAR DAUGHTER (3–9–7)	Lost, Lost
SONATINA (3–9–0)	Lost, Lost
INJAAZ (3–9–1)	Lost, Lost
PEACEFUL PARADISE (3–9–7)	Lost

Ladbroke Stakes

THE WHISTLING TEAL (5–9–3)	Won 7–1

Owen Brown Stakes
FLETCHER (7–9–0)   Won 7–2
LAFFAH (6–9–0)   Lost, Lost
MENTAL PRESSURE (8–9–0)   Won 11–4
JOHNNY OSCAR (4–9–12)   Lost, Won 7–2

33 bets, 8 winners, 25 losers. Percentage of winners: 24.2.
Profit: 1.83 points. Profit on outlay: 5.6 per cent.

Year 2

Duke of Edinburgh Stakes
HOLY ORDERS (5–9–2)   Lost, Lost
RED CARNATION (4–9–5)   Lost, Lost
TAKAMAKA BAY (5–9–4)   Lost, Lost

Balmoral Handicap
AGNETHA (3–9–7)   Won 11–2

Royal Hunt Cup
SEA STAR (4–9–6)   Lost
KELBURNE (5–9–4)   Lost, Lost

Ascot Stakes
RANDOM QUEST (4–9–7)   Won 15–8
BILLY BONNIE (5–9–0)   Lost

King George V Stakes
LEADERSHIP (3–9–0)   Lost, Won 5–2
GRAMPIAN (3–9–7)   Lost, Lost

Britannia Stakes
SHOT TO FAME (3–9–2)   Did not race
BONECRUSHER (3–9–2)   Won 7–1

Buckingham Palace Stakes
POINT OF DISPUTE (7–9–2)   Lost, Lost
SCOTTY'S FUTURE (4–9–5)   Lost, Lost

Wokingham Stakes
BORDER SUBJECT (5–9–10)   Lost, Lost
CHOOKIE HEITON (4–9–4)   Won 2–1
CRYSTAL CASTLE (4–9–4)   Won 14–1

Sandringham Rated Stakes
PURPLE HAZE (3–9–7)   Lost

26 bets, 6 winners, 20 losers. Percentage of winners: 23.1.
Profit: 12.88 points. Profit on outlay: 49.5 per cent.

Year 3

Duke of Edinburgh Stakes
RESEARCHED (4–9–10)   Lost, Won 8–1
HAMBLEDEN (6–9–4)   Lost, Lost
PAGAN DANCE (4–9–1)   Won 9–2
KING'S CONSUL (4–9–9)   Lost, Lost

Balmoral Handicap
COCONUT PENANG (3–9–3)   Lost, Lost

Royal Hunt Cup
UNSHAKABLE (4–9–2)   Lost, Lost

Ascot Stakes
LANDING LIGHT (8–10–0)   Lost, Won 12–1
MANA D'ARGENT (6–9–3)   Lost, Won 5–1

King George V Stakes
SALSALINO (3–9–2)   Lost, Lost
ETESAAL (3–9–4)   Lost
BLYTHE KNIGHT (3–9–4)   Lost, Lost

Britannia Stakes
HELM BANK (3–9–4)   Did not race
COURT MASTERPIECE (3–9–7)   Lost, Won 5–1

Wolferton Rated Stakes
BOURGAINVILLE (5–9–4)   Lost, Lost
BINARY FILE (5–9–7)   Lost, Lost

Buckingham Palace Stakes
MINE (5–9–4)   Lost, Lost

Sandringham Rated Stakes
SHARPLAW VENTURE (3–9–1)   Lost, Lost
CHIC (3–9–1)   Lost, Lost
NASU (3–9–4)   Did not race

Wokingham Stakes
RATIO (5–9–3) Dead-heat 1–2   Lost, Won 9–2
FAYR JAG (4–9–6) Dead-heat 1–2   Lost, Won 11–8
THE TATLING (6–9–6)   Lost, Won 7–2
CAPRICHO (6–9–8)   Lost

39 bets, 8 winners, 31 losers. Percentage of winners: 20.5.
Profit: 12.88 points. Profit on outlay: 33.0 per cent.

Two out of three years yielded a perfectly acceptable profit therefore, but Year 1 did less well with only a small gain overall. As with all racing systems, whether producing a limited number of selections or a comparatively large number, this variability is an inevitable part of betting according to automatic rules. However, provided the system has a sound, logical basis, the best methods more or less guarantee that the backer will not lose much even if winners do not occur in the expected numbers. This is true of the Royal Ascot Handicappers method. In fact it is not so much the number of winners indicated that matters most in systems of this kind, but their starting prices. That is an unpredictable factor over which the system bettor has no control, but the record set out above strongly suggests that there will usually be enough winners at biggish prices to offset losing stakes, and still produce a profit when the selections are taken as a whole.

As with all systems based on handicap betting, the systemite must be prepared to accept quite a few losers on the way to the winners at decent odds which ought to make a profit possible. The right sort of temperament is a prerequisite of success therefore. Readers who become discouraged easily after a run of losers should avoid the plan. Patient backers on the other hand could be well rewarded if they decide to adopt it.

Form Indicator of Winners at Glorious Goodwood

Glorious Goodwood is twinned in the minds of most racing fans with Royal Ascot as the concluding half of the summer acme of the Flat racing season. From many points of view, however, the two meetings are quite different, despite the superficial similarity. As far as betting goes, Royal Ascot has frequently proved a backers' graveyard, and may well be many times in the future. By contrast, season after season Goodwood's famous July meeting produces a stream of results which tend to confirm any sensible reading of form. Even Goodwood's many handicaps tend to fall to well-backed form candidates. Perfect ground, as well as the composition of the five-day programme, and the meeting's position in the racing year just when the good horses are reaching their peak, make Glorious Goodwood worthy of the very closest attention from serious backers of horses.

Nor in the opinion of this writer is it necessary to scratch far below the surface of form to be successful in finding plenty of winners at reasonable prices. That is because intensive research has revealed some highly significant facts about the statistical norms to which many Goodwood winners conform.

The particular form indicator discussed in this section of our chapter on racing systems turns on where runners at Glorious Goodwood ran last time out, and on what position in their race they finished, two simple guides to future performance which are especially potent in combination at this meeting, provided of course the correct conclusions have been drawn from the statistical record going back over many years. Also, it is obviously a prerequisite of success that these statistical trends should go on recurring in the future.

Here in a nutshell is the Goodwood Plan:

> *A significant number of winners at Glorious Goodwood each year were first or second last time out at one or other of just four courses, namely Ascot (Heath meetings as well as Royal Ascot), Kempton Park, Newbury or Newmarket.*
> *It is on horses which have this double qualification that backers should concentrate.*

As always, though one cannot say for sure what will happen in the future, results from the very recent past are the best evidence available of any plan's likely success. The winners which have continued to flow from this idea in the last four years surely speak volumes about what it is reasonable to expect in coming seasons. Of the years analysed, Year 4 is the most recent of all.

WINNERS AT GLORIOUS GOODWOOD, FIRST OR SECOND LAST TIME OUT AT ASCOT, KEMPTON, NEWBURY OR NEWMARKET

Year 1

		Goodwood Result	Previous Place and Venue
Tuesday	ALEXIUS	Won 7–1	Won Newmarket
Tuesday	KELBURNE	Won 9–4F	Won Ascot
Wednesday	NOVERRE	Won 9–2	2nd Ascot
Wednesday	ZUHAIR	Won 7–2F	2nd Kempton
Thursday	PERSIAN PUNCH	Won 6–1	2nd Ascot
Friday	ASKHAM	Won 11–4F	2nd Newmarket

Year 2

		Goodwood Result	Previous Place and Venue
Tuesday	TRUE NIGHT	Won 4–1F	Won Ascot
Wednesday	DUBLIN	Won 11–1	Won Newbury
Wednesday	ROCK OF GIBRALTAR	Won 8–13F	Won Ascot
Wednesday	MAMOUNIA	Won 7–2F	Won Newmarket
Wednesday	JUDHOOR	Won 2–5F	2nd Newmarket
Thursday	WUNDERS DREAM	Won 8–1	2nd Newbury
Friday	MACAW	Won 7–1	Won Newmarket
Friday	SMIRK	Won 12–1	2nd Newbury
Friday	FANCY LADY	Won 13–8F	Won Newmarket
Saturday	LOOKING DOWN	Won 8–1	2nd Ascot
Saturday	DUBAIAN GIFT	Won 11–2	2nd Kempton

Year 3

		Goodwood Result	Previous Place and Venue
Tuesday	PHOENIX REACH	Won 12–1	Won Newbury
Tuesday	TAHREEB	Won 6–4F	2nd Kempton
Wednesday	HOH BUZZARD	Won 7–2F	Won Newmarket
Thursday	ALKAADHEM	Won 4–5F	2nd Newbury
Friday	TIBER	Won 7–2F	2nd Newmarket
Friday	PSYCHIATRIST	Won 7–2	2nd Newmarket
Saturday	MOMENTS OF JOY	Won 15–2	Won Kempton
Saturday	RUSSIAN RHYTHM	Won 4–5F	Won Ascot
Saturday	PATAVELLIAN	Won 4–1	Won Newmarket

Year 4

		Goodwood Result	Previous Place and Venue
Tuesday	MARAAHEL	Won 9–4	2nd Ascot
Tuesday	MEPHISTO	Won 7–2F	Won Newmarket
Wednesday	SOVIET SONG	Won 3–1	Won Newmarket
Wednesday	CUTTING CREW	Won 12–1	2nd Ascot
Wednesday	DIAMOND LODGE	Won 11–4F	Won Newmarket
Thursday	ART TRADER	Won 7–2F	2nd Newmarket
Friday	JIMMY RYAN	Won 12–1	2nd Ascot
Saturday	FONG'S THONG	Won 6–4F	Won Newbury
Saturday	PIVOTAL POINT	Won 7–1CoF	2nd Ascot

Pivotal Point, the Stewards' Cup winner, was the sole qualifier in its race and was one of only four on the whole Saturday card. Best-priced at 14–1 in the morning, it went off at half those odds. Our method had done just as well as those 'in the know' who had instigated the gamble, a most pleasing result.

The form indicator which had produced all these winners is not, strictly speaking, a complete system in its own right. It is not suggested that backing every horse at Glorious Goodwood which meets the basic qualifications will automatically yield a profit over the five days of the meeting, although in some years that would have been the case. Year 4, for example, was such a year.

In applying the indicator it is better to use discretion about which horses to actually back, for on occasion there could be too many qualifiers overall, and there may be plenty of instances of a number of qualifiers running in the same race. However, as a starting point for picking out the most likely form horses to bet on at the Goodwood festival meeting, the methodology explained here takes some beating in respect of both its potential for finding winners and the odds available about some of them.

Form Horses in Late Summer and Early Autumn

This is a plan for the specialists who take their betting very seriously indeed and who only get involved when everything seems in their favour, although obviously its use does not preclude following other methodologies, either simultaneously or at other times.

It is used for only three months of the year, the three months when the normal bias in horse racing is reversed and conditions favour, not the bookmaker, but the backer. These three months are July, August and September – July and August on the Flat, and August and September over the jumps.

Up to July, Flat form is variable in the extreme. Fitness

is hard to assess early in the season. As competition hots up in May and June, bigger fields and the gradual appearance of better-class animals tend to produce reversals in form and plenty of shock results. During July and August on the other hand, form is much more settled. Also, fast ground produces small fields. Form horses starting favourite go in with pleasing regularity in certain kinds of race. Come September, however, the situation changes again. The going eases, fields swell and many horses have gone off the boil with too much racing and are at a serious disadvantage against late-maturing, autumn types. Form once more becomes unreliable and inconsistent.

August and September similarly are the backers' months in National Hunt racing. By August the new jumping season is well under way, but only a few jumpers can really handle the firm ground. The result is small fields dominated by fit horses which have conditions ideal for them. Starting prices are on the short side but four or five winning favourites at a meeting is a commonplace event. In October the jumping season 'proper' starts. There should have been enough rain to allow the genuine winter types to make their bow and, therefore, the pendulum swings back to the bookmaker with the beginning of the long haul of intense competition which leads up to Cheltenham in March.

In July this system operates on the Flat only. August allows a mixture of bets from both codes of racing. In September, selections come exclusively from the jumping sphere.

Three horses a day are selected and backed in three singles, three doubles and a treble in a daily seven-point wager. All selections are drawn from non-handicaps, and only market horses with a clear form advantage are good enough. Within reason the backer should not shy away from the inclusion of some odds-on chances. The aim is to land three winners in a day for successful doubles, crowned by a treble, and winners are more important than prices. On the Flat it is a good idea to ignore the principal meeting of the day if there are plenty of opportunities elsewhere. Generally speaking it is easier to find winners at lowly Thirsk or Yarmouth than at glamorous York or Ascot, just as the likes of Sedgefield and Newton Abbot offer relatively easy pickings for the discerning student of National Hunt form at the appropriate time of year.

The mathematics of the plan are straightforward enough. Around 50 per cent of winners each week should see the bet holding its own overall and, given the circumstances governing selections, such a percentage is easily within reach of any competent racing enthusiast. Profits will accrue from those days when all three selections win. If operators of the plan can turn up an average of only one successful treble each week, they ought to be well in pocket at the end of the three months of betting.

The system is subject to the vicissitudes of horse racing like any other gamble on the sport, but it is a low risk 'bread and butter' plan. For the patient punter who is prepared to hammer away at this particular chink in the bookmakers' armour, there may be plenty of 'jam' too.

A Plan for Nursery Handicaps

Specialisation pays in betting on horses, and specialisation is most effective when it is linked to a particular category of race at a particular time of year.

Nursery handicaps are a good example. The two-year-old handicap season begins in late July when the ground is fast and two-year-old form is exposed, at least for the class of animal that habitually competes in this type of event. Later on, in September and afterwards, late-season debutants begin to participate, and form lines established early in the year come into conflict with the form of the later arrivals. After August, as the rains arrive and form is much more complex to unravel, nurseries become a far less favourable medium for backers looking for a steady profit from fancied two-year-olds.

Here then are the rules for our Nursery Plan:

1   Bet only from the beginning of the nursery season in the last days of July to the end of August.

2   Select only winners last time out provided they are quoted in the first four in the betting forecast of the newspaper used for betting purposes.

3   There can be a maximum of two selections per race. If more than two horses in the first four in the betting forecast won last time out, take the two at the shortest prices. If there is only one winner last time out in the first four betting quotes, that is the sole selection for the race.

4   Stakes are 1 point on each qualifier. Therefore, where there is a single selection, the stake is 1 point on the race. Where there are two qualifiers in a race, the stakes are 1 point on each selection, that is 2 points for the race.

On the next page are the results for the most recent season at the time of writing. It can be seen that although there are plenty of losers, the percentage of winners is sound, and starting prices are good enough to produce an excellent overall profit.

		Profit (+) or Loss (−) on race	Total Profit (+) or Loss (−)
30/7/03	JUST ONE LOOK (13–2); Loser	+£5.50	+£5.50
1/8/03	BLUE TOMATO (7–2)	+£3.50	+£9.00
2/8/03	Loser; Loser	−£2.00	+£7.00
2/8/03	BENTLEY'S BALL (3–1); Loser	+£2.00	+£9.00
2/8/03	CAPE TRAFALGAR (5–1)	+£5.00	+£14.00
3/8/03	PEAK TO CREEK (13–8); Loser	+£0.63	+£14.63
3/8/03	GO BANANAS (5–2)	+£2.50	+£17.13
7/8/03	Loser	−£1.00	+£16.13
8/8/03	SUTTER'S FORT (5–2); Loser	+£1.50	+£17.63
8/8/03	Loser	−£1.00	+£16.63
11/8/03	HILITES (9–2); Loser	+£3.50	+£20.13
14/8/03	WHISPERED PROMISES (11–4); Loser	+£1.75	+£21.88
14/8/03	Loser	−£1.00	+£20.88
14/8/03	Loser	−£1.00	+£19.88
15/8/03	Loser	−£1.00	+£18.88
15/8/03	MANIPULATOR (2–1); Loser	+£1.00	+£19.88
16/8/03	MOLCON (13–2)	+£6.50	+£26.38
17/8/03	MAC LOVE (7–2); Loser	+£2.50	+£28.88
18/8/03	BONNE DE FLEUR (5–1); Loser	+£4.00	+£32.88
19/8/03	BLUE TOMATO (15–8); Loser	+£0.88	+£33.76
21/8/03	PERFECT DISTANCE (7–2); Loser	+£2.50	+£36.26
21/8/03	Loser; Loser	−£2.00	+£34.26
22/8/03	TOP SPEC (3–1); Loser	+£2.00	+£36.26
23/8/03	DIOSYPROS BLUE (11–4); Loser	+£1.75	+£38.01
24/8/03	Loser; Loser	−£2.00	+£36.01
24/8/03	MADAEH (8–13); Loser	−£0.38	+£35.63
25/8/03	Loser; Loser	−£2.00	+£33.63
25/8/03	HAPPY CRUSADER (10–11); Loser	−£0.09	+£33.54
25/8/03	Loser; Loser	−£2.00	+£31.54
27/8/03	DIOSYPROS BLUE (15–8); Loser	+£0.88	+£32.42
28/8/03	Loser	−£1.00	+£31.42
29/8/03	ASIA (10–11)	+£0.91	+£32.33
30/8/03	Loser; Loser	−£2.00	+£30.33

Thus there was a total of 55 bets, of which 21 won and 34 lost, a 38.2 per cent strike rate of winners. The profit on stakes of £55 was £30.33, a yield of 55.2 per cent profit on total outlay.

Although nothing is guaranteed in racing and betting, it is reasonable to expect a similar successful return for the plan in the seasons to come. A good percentage of winners is highly probable and, in handicaps for two-year-olds, starting prices even for fancied horses should be high enough overall to carry the sequence into profit.

A Key Race to Backend Profits

The final months of the Flat, as we have already seen, can be difficult ones for backers. Autumn brings changes in the going and big fields, and it is so easy for even the most conservative of punters to let a good spring and summer profit slip away. A proven method that holds out real prospects of boosting earlier gains must be worth its weight in gold to the discerning racing enthusiast.

The following simple system has an excellent record over many years and, though it may not produce a gain every season, it is statistically fair odds-on that it will finish on the right side. Like all sound racing plans, it is founded on racing logic in tune with conditions that suit a particular type of horse at a particular time of year.

The idea is to list the first five home in the biggest sprint at Glorious Goodwood, the Stewards' Cup. The race is run over six furlongs on the Saturday of the July/August meeting and features the best sprint handicappers in training. In the weeks that follow, the Racing Calendar is full of sprints in which horses that have run well in the race can be exploited, over the minimum trip as well as over six or even seven furlongs. Thus there is no danger of the clashing in the same races that bedevils many plans based on a list of horses to follow. With plenty of sprints to aim at in the final weeks of the Flat, horses which went close in the Stewards' Cup have many opportunities to go in at good prices.

There is always one big problem for system backers who list horses and back them each time they run. However well the horses in the list are doing as a group, quite often there is one animal that chalks up a long sequence of losing races, thereby eating away at the gains from more successful qualifiers. As a safeguard against this scenario, therefore, each of the five listed horses from the Stewards' Cup are backed in their next three outings only. Then, win or lose overall, they are deleted from the list. So the method costs a maximum of just 15 points per year at level stakes.

Sprinters, less than staying horses, do not race abroad all that much. As already noted, there are so many races for them in Britain that expensive trips abroad are just not necessary for stables in search of prize money. However, if you are a keen student of racing who follows events in Ireland and France closely, especially at the weekends, the record indicates that it will pay to back qualifiers when they do leave our shores. The wisdom of such a policy was underlined in the season just ended as I write, when Patavellian, the winner of the Stewards' Cup, turned up at Longchamp for the Prix de l'Abbaye and won at a highly rewarding 9–1.

Here is the complete record of the system qualifiers for the last three seasons. Year 3 is the most recent of the three.

Year 1

GUINEA HUNTER	Lost, Lost, Lost
HALMAHERA	Lost, Lost, Lost
UNDETERRED	Lost, Lost, Lost
PERFECT PEACH	Lost, Lost, Lost
HONESTY FAIR	Lost, Lost, Won 7–1

Profit/Loss: –7 points

The overall result would have looked very different had Perfect Peach won instead of being beaten a head at 20–1 in a Listed race at Pontefract on its next run after finishing fourth in the Stewards' Cup. However, the following two seasons made up for this near miss:

Year 2

BOND BOY	Lost, Lost, Won 12–1
HALMAHERA	Lost, Lost, Won 6–1
UNDETERRED	Lost, Lost, Lost
HURRICANE FLOYD	Lost, Lost, Lost
TAYIF	Lost, Lost, Lost

Profit/Loss: +5 points

Year 3

PATAVELLIAN	Won 9–1
FIRE UP THE BAND	Lost, Lost, Lost
COLONEL COTTON	Lost, Lost, Won 25–1
FRIZZANTE	Lost, Won 10–11, Won 11–10
ONLYTIME WILL TELL	Lost, Lost

Profit/Loss: +28.01 points

With such a small group of horses, and a maximum of 15 bets in a series, profits are bound to be variable, and the possibility of the occasional losing season cannot be discounted. It is tempting, given the number of system qualifiers which finished in a place at good odds, to make the plan an each-way one, but Rule 3 of the *12 Golden Rules of Successful Betting* set out later in this book, should demonstrate that in the long run this is not a wise policy. Plenty of placed horses at long odds give the punter reassurance that all is well, but sticking to win-only bets will usually come out on top in the end.

Dependent as it is on an occasional long-priced winner from a relatively small number of bets spread over just a few weeks, the plan outlined above may never be more than just one part of a much bigger betting strategy.

Nevertheless, for anyone with the discipline needed to wait out the losers, reinforced by faith in the idea as a long-term profit-maker, there is a distinct chance that the Stewards' Cup can be turned into a way of winning money from a select group of horses during the autumn of each Flat racing season.

Speed Horses on the All-Weather Tracks

Quite apart from the difference in surfaces as a result of which the same horse is quite likely to show a completely different level of ability on sand compared with its effectiveness on turf, analysis of form on the all-weather tracks in Britain is a separate and distinct problem from the assessment of form in conventional grass-track racing.

To begin with, weight counts for little even in handicaps on the all-weather. Pace on the other hand is vitally important. In most turf races the pace builds up steadily until the final two furlongs or so when the leading contenders all start to sprint for the line at approximately the same time. In all-weather racing on the other hand the pace is much more uniform throughout a contest. The pace may be fast or slow, comparatively speaking, but there is much less of a helter-skelter sprint at the end of races.

Until sectional times are available in the UK by which form students can compare the pace at different points in the race, and particularly in the final two or three furlongs relative to its opening and middle sections, the British punter has no real clue as to variations in pace in all-weather contests.

However, comparisons against standard times for course and distance are just as possible for the all-weather as for grass, and speed figures that measure the overall time of a horse in a race are highly relevant for predicting future results, arguably much more relevant than for turf events. Both the racing trade daily and weekly racing publications give speed figures for the all-weather, and these should be the punter's main resource in analysing races on sand.

Here are a set of simple, time-based rules which can be applied to the three all-weather tracks currently operating in the UK:

1   Examine only winners last time out running within approximately 21 days of their previous outing. In their latest run, potential bets should have recorded their fastest speed figure for some time. Weight on the occasion of their previous run or in today's race should not form part of the speed-figure assessment. It is the raw time for a race measured against the standard for course and distance, with a going correction as incorporated in all published speed figures, that is important.

2   There should be a minimum standard for a speed figure to qualify a horse for a bet. So if, barring freak results, the highest rating of the best all-weather horses is in the 115 zone, any horse recording a speed figure of something over 100 would be worthy of consideration, if that is its best figure for some time.

3   To qualify, a horse need not necessarily have the highest figure in the race under review, but its figure should be at least within five per cent of so of the top-rated speed horse in the race. Thus if the best speed figure of any of its opponents is, say, 110, it must have recorded at least a figure of 110 minus $(110 \times \frac{5}{100}) = 5.5$ points, that is, a figure of 104 or 105.

The other highly significant factor in all-weather racing is the draw. On some grass tracks the draw is obviously important too, but on the all-weather at Lingfield, Southwell and Wolverhampton, the draw generally has a huge effect on results. There are exceptions to every rule of course, but no bet on the all-weather should be struck before ascertaining that the horse in question has a favourable draw that will give it an advantage over at least some, if not most, of its competitors.

Therefore the final part of our speed-figure system for the all-weather is to restrict wagers to horses which are well drawn according to the following specifications for each of the three tracks:

LINGFIELD
1   Bet only in races with 11 or more runners.
2   Bet only in races of from 5 to 10 furlongs inclusive.
3   Bet only if a speed horse identified above as a potential wager is *one of the four lowest drawn* horses in the race.

SOUTHWELL
1   Bet only in races with 11 or more runners.
2   Bet only in races of from six furlongs to one mile three furlongs inclusive.
3   Bet only if a speed horse indicated above as a potential bet is one of the *four lowest drawn* horses in the race.

WOLVERHAMPTON
1   Bet only in races with 11 or more runners.
2   Bet only in races from five furlongs to one mile one and a half furlongs inclusive.
3   Bet only if a speed horse indicated above as a possible wager is *one of the six highest drawn* horses in the race.*

*The reshaping of the bends which has accompanied the laying down of the new Polytrack at Wolverhampton may mean that the advantage to middle to high numbers may not be confirmed after the beginning of October 2004.

All this may seem horribly complicated at first glance, but really it is only a case of applying the rules in logical sequence to arrive at a bet, although some element of interpretation may be required in the analysis of speed figures.

Just how simple and effective the plan can be was highlighted by racing on the all-weather track at Lingfield on Saturday, 28 February 2004.

One horse on the card caught the eye immediately. This was Consonant, which was down to run in a one-mile-two-furlongs handicap. It had won its last three races on the all-weather since leaving a famous Turf stable and had recorded the following speed figures:

108 (previous run) 87 (penultimate run) 111 (latest run)

Though its speed form had dipped in the middle of its winning sequence, this showed versatility. The horse could win off a slow as well as a fast pace. A latest figure of 111 was excellent, and some 12 points higher than the horse's nearest rival on time, Moayed.

Consonant was also drawn 3 of the 14 runners, to make it a stand-out bet.

Later on the same card was Forever Phoenix which was running in a six-furlong handicap at the Surrey track. Its speed figures were:

98 (previous run) 95 (penultimate run) 103 (latest run)

Again there was evidence of improvement in the figures, and its rating of 103 when it won 11 days previously indicated that the horse might well be capable of achieving its best rating of the previous season of 107 now that it had hit form. Its nearest speed rival was Miss Poppets with a figure of 104. In addition, Forever Phoenix was drawn number 1 in the field of 11 runners.

Here were two sound bets for the system, with Consonant looking especially attractive as a betting proposition. When it was also noted that the redoubtable champion jockey, Kieren Fallon was to ride Consonant, and that crack Irishman, Johnny Murtagh, would be in the plate on Forever Phoenix, there were good grounds for extra confidence. For there can be no doubt that in a dash from pillar to post around a bend, the presence of a top jockey in the saddle can make all the difference to a horse's chance on the all-weather circuits. This should always be borne in mind when making selections. Fallon, M. Dwyer, D. Holland, J. Fanning and J.P. Spencer currently head the all-weather percentages, but the comparatively rare appearances of a Murtagh, a Dettori or a Richard Hughes on a horse racing on sand should always make one sit up and take notice.

In the case of Consonant and Forever Phoenix, the indications of the speed system, reinforced by the bookings of two of the most talented Irish jockeys riding at present, turned out to be spot on. Consonant won at 5–1, Forever Phoenix at 3–1, and this author's two singles and a double landed the biggest coup he had pulled off in many a month.

That day also underlined the great significance of the draw, particularly at Lingfield. Here are the results for the whole card, with the race distance shown first, followed by the stall occupied by the winner, and then the number of runners in each race.

	Draw	
5f	10	10 ran
1m	4	9 ran
10f	2	14 ran
10f	3	14 ran
10f	7	14 ran
6f	1	11 ran
7f	4	13 ran
13f	1	12 ran

With the exception of the first race in which the favourite, Polish Emperor, drawn 1, was beaten a head by Turibius, who was given a brilliant ride by Kieren Fallon from the outside stall, all the races on this day went to horses in the bottom half of the draw, and most were won by those in stalls 1 to 4. The meeting therefore provided a sound justification for one of the system rules. On this Saturday at Lingfield in February, as at all meetings at Lingfield on the all-weather circuit, low-drawn horses in biggish fields have much the best of the results.

The draw and speed are the keys to all-weather racing at the three courses where it currently takes place. Plans are in the offing for new all-weather venues. Those prepared to study this sphere of racing now and in the future along the lines indicated above have every prospect of finding plenty of winners at rewarding prices.

Favourites and Outsiders at the Cheltenham Festival

The year 2003 was an exceptional one at the Cheltenham Festival. In the 20 races that are spread over the three days of the meeting, a record number of 10 favourites won. Everyone who made the journey to the Cotswolds claimed to have returned home a big winner and, if the press are to be believed, the bookmakers took the biggest pasting in human memory.

How different to so many other Cheltenhams when intense competition among the best jumpers in training produces shock result after shock result, and horror stories abound of seasoned punters failing to back a winner throughout the three days. In many years, it seems, only the Irish have automatic cause for celebration, though in their case a win for a horse from the Emerald Isle is reason enough to shout the roof of the stands down, whether they actually backed their equine compatriot or not. For lots of other punters who measure their success less patriotically in terms of profit or loss, Cheltenham can be a nightmare, and if the occasion itself is to be enjoyed and savoured, that is too often a pleasure to be paid for by the sight of hard cash flowing into the bookies' satchels and staying there.

Yet even the most difficult of Cheltenhams need not be a backer's graveyard. The key, as is the case with so much in betting on horses, is to be selective. There are just a few races on the annual programme whose conditions actually favour well-backed runners and, while these events can never be described as a punters' benefit in the way that so many other races at the Festival are a bookmakers' benefit, stakes on favourites, properly planned, may well come to one's rescue, even if more speculative punts go awry.

Here is a select list of the best races for favourites at the Cheltenham Festival. Not every favourite will win in any one year of course, but taken together these contests represent a corpus of races in which the horses with the best public form are most likely to succeed. This is borne out by statistics. The most recent of the six seasons analysed is Year 6, in the extreme right-hand column of the table. Apart from successful favourites, winning second or third favourites are also shown to indicate that wins for the favourites are not isolated instances, but that the chosen events are generally good for well-backed horses. Where a race was won by a horse outside the first three in the racecourse betting, this is shown by a dash.

CHELTENHAM FESTIVAL –
BEST RACES FOR FAVOURITES

	Year 1	Year 2	Year 3	Year 4	Year 5	Year 6
Supreme Novices' Hurdle (Tuesday)	2nd F	2nd F	—	**7–4F**	**3–1F**	**7–2F**
Champion Hurdle (Tuesday)	**3–1F**	**4–9F**	**8–15F**	—	2nd F	—
Royal & SunAlliance Novices' Hurdle (Wednesday)	**2–1F**	**2–1F**	**5–4F**	—	3rd F	—
Queen Mother Champion Chase (Wednesday)	3rd F	2nd F	2nd F	**7–4F**	**7–4F**	2nd F
Stayers' Hurdle (Thursday)	—	—	3rd F	**13–8F**	**9–4JF**	2nd F
Cheltenham Grand Annual Chase Challenge Cup (Thursday)	**7–2F**	**7–2F**	**9–2F**	2nd F	—	**4–1F**
Cathcart Challenge Cup Chase (Thursday)	**9–4F**	—	3rd F	**2–1F**	**5–4F**	—

In these races, therefore, all is not doom and gloom for the backer – very far from it. There was in fact a level-stakes profit every year, as follows:

ANNUAL LEVEL-STAKES PROFIT
One point each favourite

Year 1	+7.75 pts.
Year 2	+1.94 pts.
Year 3	+2.28 pts.
Year 4	+4.13 pts.
Year 5	+3.63 pts.
Year 6	+2.50 pts.

There is nothing to get wildly excited about here perhaps but, when it is considered that there were only seven bets in each series, the figures are indicative of the soundness of the selected races as a medium for backing favourites. Certainly the returns belie the notion that every Cheltenham Festival is a disaster waiting to happen for the punter.

Also, a staking plan might well enhance profits. Whereas in the Classics sequences shown earlier on page 89 only one favourite in five could be counted on, here there is a minimum of two successful favourites from seven races even in the worst year. So there is no need to increase stakes after losers as in the Classic series. With a minimum expectancy of two winners out of seven, a much safer policy of increasing stakes only after a winner can be adopted.

Here is what happens if the backer stakes one point on the first favourite in the sequence and increases the bet to two points when a winner is found. Since two winning favourites is a historical minimum, betting could terminate there. This is the outcome:

CHELTENHAM FAVOURITES
One point to win. Increase by one point after a winner.
Stop after two winners.

Year 1

Supreme Novices'	Lost	−1.00
Champion Hurdle	Won 3–1	+3.00
Royal & SunAlliance	Won 2–1	+4.00
		Profit: +6.00 pts.

Year 2

Supreme Novices'	Lost	−1.00
Champion Hurdle	Won 4–9	+0.44
Royal & SunAlliance	Won 2–1	+4.00
		Profit: +3.44 pts.

Year 3

Supreme Novices'	Lost	−1.00
Champion Hurdle	Won 8–15	+0.53
Royal & SunAlliance	Won 5–4	+2.50
		Profit: +2.03 pts.

Year 4

Supreme Novices'	Won 7–4	+1.75
Champion Hurdle	Lost	−2.00
Royal & SunAlliance	Lost	−2.00
Queen Mother	Won 7–4	+3.50
		Profit: +1.25 pts.

Year 5

Supreme Novices'	Won 3–1	+3.00
Champion Hurdle	Lost	−2.00
Royal & SunAlliance	Lost	−2.00
Queen Mother	Won 7–4	+3.50
		Profit: +2.50 pts.

Year 6

Supreme Novices'	Won 7–2	+3.50
Champion Hurdle	Lost	−2.00
Royal & SunAlliance	Lost	−2.00
Queen Mother	Lost	−2.00
Stayers' Hurdle	Lost	−2.00
Grand Annual	Won 4–1	+8.00
		Profit: +3.50 pts.

In fact, level stakes did slightly better than the staking plan. Over the six years, level stakes yielded an overall gain of 22.23 points, but the staking system produced a profit of only 18.72 points. Although different patterns of results and prices will give different outcomes, there seems little mileage in risking the extra point per race after the first winner.

However, let us see what happens when the stop-at-two-wins proviso is dropped altogether.

CHELTENHAM FAVOURITES
One point to win. Increase by one point after each winner.

Year 1

Supreme Novices'	Lost	−1.00
Champion Hurdle	Won 3–1	+3.00
Royal & SunAlliance	Won 2–1	+4.00
Queen Mother	Lost	−3.00
Stayers' Hurdle	Lost	−3.00
Grand Annual	Won 7–2	+10.50
Cathcart	Won 9–4	+9.00
		Profit: +19.50 pts.

Year 2

Supreme Novices'	Lost	−1.00
Champion Hurdle	Won 4–9	+0.44
Royal & SunAlliance	Won 2–1	+4.00
Queen Mother	Lost	−3.00
Stayers' Hurdle	Lost	−3.00
Grand Annual	Won 7–2	+10.50
Cathcart	Lost	−4.00
		Profit: +3.94 pts.

Year 3

Supreme Novices'	Lost	−1.00
Champion Hurdle	Won 8–15	+0.53
Royal & SunAlliance	Won 5–4	+2.50
Queen Mother	Lost	−3.00
Stayers' Hurdle	Lost	−3.00
Grand Annual	Won 9–2	+13.50
Cathcart	Lost	−4.00
		Profit: +5.53 pts.

Year 4

Supreme Novices'	Won 7–4	+1.75
Champion Hurdle	Lost	–2.00
Royal & SunAlliance	Lost	–2.00
Queen Mother	Won 7–4	+3.50
Stayers' Hurdle	Won 13–8	+4.88
Grand Annual	Lost	–4.00
Cathcart	Won 2–1	+8.00
		Profit: +10.13 pts.

Year 5

Supreme Novices'	Won 3–1	+3.00
Champion Hurdle	Lost	–2.00
Royal & SunAlliance	Lost	–2.00
Queen Mother	Won 7–4	+3.50
Stayers' Hurdle	Won 9–4JF	+1.88
Grand Annual	Lost	–4.00
Cathcart	Won 5–4	+5.00
		Profit: +5.38 pts.

Year 6

Supreme Novices'	Won 7–2	+3.50
Champion Hurdle	Lost	–2.00
Royal & SunAlliance	Lost	–2.00
Queen Mother	Lost	–2.00
Stayers' Hurdle	Lost	–2.00
Grand Annual	Won 4–1	+8.00
Cathcart	Lost	–3.00
		Profit: +0.50 pts.

Thus, at the risk of sacrificing profits if a third winner is not forthcoming (Year 6, for example), modification of the staking plan has increased the overall profit to no less than 44.98 points. True, staking was at a higher level, but since bets were only increased after a winner, this was largely self-financing. Even when betting continued beyond the second winner, at no point in any of the sequences would the backer have been more than 4.50 points down (Year 6 again, after the Stayers' Hurdle). As a result of using money won from the bookmaker, this slight increase in capital at risk compared with level stakes was more than justified by the enhanced gain that accrued.

That said, there is a downside. It is perfectly possible – not likely but still possible – that all seven favourites could be beaten in the same year. Yet even here the benefits of increasing stakes after a winner are revealed, for the total loss on a series would only come to seven points, exactly the same amount as if the backer had stuck to level stakes all along. If, however, a very short-priced winner, say, odds-on, won early in a sequence and no other winners were found, this would call for a two-point stake on the remaining races, and that would increase the backer's liability beyond the basic seven points. It is very seldom that one can have everything when gambling on horses, and it is only fair to readers to point out this less desirable scenario. In fact any lone winner, even one at a good price for a favourite, could produce a final deficit in excess of seven points if it occurs early enough in the sequence, thereby triggering double stakes on losers in the remaining races, which will be in a majority.

So much for favourites. What about outsiders? At such a cosmopolitan meeting involving big fields and so many good horses, it is hardly surprising that no distinct, repeating form patterns are discernible, but there is one simple little plan that has worked in the past, and may continue to do so as long as Martin Pipe remains pre-eminent in the ranks of National Hunt trainers.

Pipe, for so long the champion trainer over jumps, may not have the potential winners of the Champion Hurdle, Queen Mother Champion Chase and the Gold Cup in his yard every year – that would be impossible; but he does always have a number of proven handicap chasers available to him, the best of which can be aimed at some of Cheltenham's lesser prizes with every chance of success, as long as they are competing at their own level.

In fact, there are only four handicap chases at the Festival. They are as follows:

William Hill National Hunt Handicap Chase (Tuesday)
Fulke Walwyn Kim Muir Challenge Cup Handicap Chase (Tuesday)
Mildmay of Flete Challenge Cup Handicap Chase (Wednesday)
Cheltenham Grand Annual Chase Challenge Cup (Thursday)

Since all are handicaps, the trainer's skill at placing his charges to best advantage comes vitally into play. The Pipe strategy is to attack these Cheltenham races in force. For those who have no difficulty with bulk betting on a great many horses in the same race, there has been no more straightforward way of picking up a profit at the Festival than to back every Martin Pipe runner in the above races with a level stake.

Here is a five-season record of how the idea would have fared in practice. Year 5 is the most recent season of all.

MARTIN PIPE RUNNERS IN
CHELTENHAM HANDICAP CHASES

Year 1
William Hill National Hunt Handicap Chase

BLOWING WIND	8–1	unplaced

Fulke Walwyn Kim Muir Challenge Cup Handicap Chase

MOONDIGUA	10–1	unplaced
PRINCE SORINIERES	16–1	unplaced
ENIVRANT	20–1	unplaced

Mildmay of Flete Challenge Cup Handicap Chase

UPGRADE	7–1	unplaced
DARK STRANGER	**14–1**	**WON**
NORTHERN STARLIGHT	14–1	unplaced

Cheltenham Grand Annual Chase Challenge Cup

CARANDREW	12–1	unplaced

Profit to 1 point all runners: 7 points

Year 2
Festival meeting abandoned.

Year 3

William Hill National Hunt Handicap Chase

YOU'RE AGOODUN	20–1	4th
TAKE CONTROL	20–1	unplaced
ROYAL PREDICA	25–1	unplaced

Fulke Walwyn Kim Muir Challenge Cup Handicap Chase

NOCKSY	10–1	unplaced
CADOUGOLD	25–1	3rd

Mildmay of Flete Challenge Cup Handicap Chase

LADY CRICKET	5–2	2nd
L'EPICUREAN	9–1	unplaced
MAJADOU	20–1	unplaced
BLOWING WIND	**25–1**	**WON**
DARK STRANGER	40–1	unplaced
TANGO ROYAL	40–1	unplaced

Cheltenham Grand Annual Chase Challenge Cup

EXIT SWINGER	4–1	2nd

Profit to 1 point all runners: 14 points

Year 4

William Hill National Hunt Handicap Chase

IZNOGOUD	9–1	unplaced
ROYAL AUCLAIR	20–1	unplaced

Fulke Walwyn Kim Muir Challenge Cup Handicap Chase

MONTREAL	12–1	unplaced
BURLU	20–1	unplaced
CARRYONHARRY	20–1	unplaced
ROYAL PREDICA	**33–1**	**WON**

Mildmay of Flete Challenge Cup Handicap Chase

LADY CRICKET	8–1	unplaced
HORUS	14–1	unplaced
BLOWING WIND	20–1	unplaced
TRESOR DE MAI	25–1	unplaced

Cheltenham Grand Annual Chase Challenge Cup

GOLDEN ALPHA	10–1	unplaced

EXIT SWINGER	14–1	unplaced

Profit to 1 point all runners: 22 points

Year 5

William Hill National Hunt Handicap Chase

CHICUELO	16–1	unplaced
YOU'RE AGOODUN	25–1	unplaced
DARK STRANGER	50–1	unplaced

Fulke Walwyn Kim Muir Challenge Cup Handicap Chase

TOTO TOSCATO	8–1	unplaced
MONDIAL JACK	10–1	unplaced
HORUS	12–1	unplaced
ROYAL PREDICA	14–1	unplaced
MONTREAL	33–1	unplaced
MAXIMIZE	**40–1**	**WON**
SULPHUR SPRINGS	66–1	unplaced

Mildmay of Flete Challenge Cup Handicap Chase

IZNOGOUD	9–2	2nd
POLAR RED	20–1	unplaced

Cheltenham Grand Annual Chase Challenge Cup

SEEBALD	12–1	unplaced
LATALOMNE	14–1	unplaced
WAHIBA SANDS	33–1	unplaced
HIT AND RUN	50–1	unplaced
TANGO ROYAL	50–1	unplaced

Profit to 1 point all runners: 24 points

Seven points, 14 points, 22 points, 24 points! How easy racing can be if one can find a really good trend and capitalise on it.

At this point something should be said about the difference between the above kind of betting which may be called bulk betting, and betting on a much smaller group against the field as explained in Chapter 5.

In group betting the idea is to convert odds to percentages. This makes possible a calculation whereby all the horses backed will return the same profit if any of them win. The point of arranging stakes to achieve this objective is to even out the difference between the odds of the horses backed, so that short-priced horses will be not less favoured than those at more speculative odds. Since the shorter-priced runners have the best chance of winning, it is important that they are accorded at least equal status with outsiders in the final wager.

In bulk betting, on the other hand, a larger number of horses for the most part are backed with the express hope of finding a winner at a big price. Since the punter wants to achieve full value for any winning outsider he or she finds, there should be no question of evening things up at its expense, so that the few horses at shorter prices will return the same amount of profit as the longshots. Therefore, level stakes are placed on all horses backed.

Bulk betting is often operated by shrewd gamblers in the hope of taking advantage of a strong statistical trend. In this example it is the consistent success of Martin Pipe in a very small set of races of a certain type at the Festival. Another example might be where a statistical backer has reason to believe from the historical record that a horse within a fairly narrow price band will win a big handicap. All those runners priced at between 12–1 and 20–1 might be backed at level stakes. If, say, there are eight such horses, and seven lose, but one wins, the backer will be well in pocket – at least five points and possibly thirteen.

This kind of punting is not new. It still has its adherents and it can enjoy a lot of success whenever statistics are borne out by results.

For many conventional punters, however, it may well go against the grain to bet on quite so many horses in the same race as in some of the races for our Pipe system. Unaware of the strategy until now, maybe they would not wish to be seen betting in what some in their ignorance might regard as a suicidal way. To admit to having backed half a dozen or more in a race could be the occasion of a few laughs and raised eyebrows among friends and acquaintances. Yet bulk betting is a recognised, if not generally known, betting technique. To those readers who have qualms about appearing eccentric, the author would say, 'Go ahead, make a fool of yourself. Back seven horses in one race, and collect your money from a 40–1 winner, as I did.'

Also, some readers may dislike betting on historical patterns generated by favourites in the manner explained in the first part of this section. It may be that they will be happiest doing what they have always done – picking out their selections and hoping for the best. Yet even for them there is an old trick known to veteran Cheltenhamites which could help them to make the right choices.

Horses which run well at the Cheltenham Festival one year quite often do so again the next. Specifically, concentrate on those animals which ran first or second at the previous Festival. It will be a surprise if the relatively short list of qualifiers does not contain at least some of the Cheltenham winners 12 months later. In the year in which I am writing there were Hardy Eustace (won 33–1), Well Chief (won 9–1), Iris's Gift (won 9–2), Azertyuiop (won 15–8), not to mention the now immortal Gold Cup winner, Best Mate. In the previous year too, Best Mate was a repeat winner, as were Rooster Booster, Baracouda and Moscow Flyer.

Cheltenham will always be one of the most difficult meetings of the year, if not the most difficult, at least for as long as it remains in its present form, and it is hoped that the ideas I have just outlined will at the very least inspire readers with the positive attitude that is always necessary if formidable challenges of any kind are to be overcome. If you like an idea for sound, logical reasons, and have faith that it will work for you, then there is always a strong possibility that it will.

Racing Profile of a Typical Grand National Winner

Most people with only a passing interest in horse racing would probably nominate the Grand National as the most difficult race of all in which to find the winner. This is certainly true in one sense, for however good the credentials of a National candidate it is statistically odds-on that the horse will not complete the course, so formidable and numerous are the fences to be negotiated in a huge field. On the other hand, the Aintree marathon is seldom won by anything but a certain type of runner with a distinct chance on form.

In fact the records show quite clearly that most Grand National winners have constants in their form which are typical of nearly all of them. As with the Derby, the racing profile of a National winner set out below will be badly wide of the mark from time to time. Horse racing is too unpredictable a sport for it to be otherwise. Also, in most years an element of interpretation in applying the profile will be required. However, all that said, analysis of the greatest gamble in steeplechasing can be remarkably accurate, provided some time is given to sifting through the evidence in order to match up the racing records of the runners with the factors which are known to bear on the race and influence its likely result. Here, the purchase of weekly racing publications with their in-depth form supplements will cut down on the work.

There are three positive factors in the profile of a typical National winner which are of major significance. They are as follows:

1 **Weight**
    Concentrate on horses carrying between 11st 5lb and 10st inclusive, and of the latter include only those whose 'long handicap' weight is 9st 8lb or more. Horses with an official rating of less than that,

but which must carry the minimum allowed weight in the race of 10st, are automatically disadvantaged. Quite apart from having to carry more weight in the handicap than they should, horses with a long handicap weight below 9st 8lb hardly ever have the class to win.

Details of the long handicap and of the official weight ratings on which it is based are given in the *Racing Post* and are on display in all betting shops. They can also be found in weekly racing papers.

2 Stamina

Include only those horses which have been placed (won, 2nd, 3rd) in a chase of 3¼ miles or further in the current season.

Even some quite serious racing fans will probably be surprised to learn that this factor will eliminate over half the field in a typical year. The ability to stay, however, is obviously a must for the race. Not many contenders will have competed over a distance close to the four and a half miles of the National itself, but to have a real chance a horse must have realistic pretensions to be more of a long-distance performer than the average three-mile chaser.

3 Odds

Contrary to popular belief, the Grand National is not an outsiders' race. In the last 20 years, only three winners have started at longer than 28–1 and, of the remainder, no fewer than 14 were priced at 16–1 or less. By looking at the prices of the big bookmakers in the press or on television on the morning of the race, therefore, it will be possible to cut out more than half the runners by the application of a very simple rule. Only horses quoted at 28–1 or less satisfy the third main positive for the race.

The problem quotation is 33–1. One winner in the 20-year period actually started at those odds, and obviously the betting market fluctuates between Saturday morning and the 'off' in mid-afternoon. Some readers might choose to include horses quoted at 33–1 as a positive just in case a reduction in price puts a horse into the main qualifying range by the time the final starting prices are calculated. Although too many exceptions are not a good idea in an exercise of this kind, this makes some statistical sense; for it could be that the strict '28–1 or under' statistic might be slightly off key with a winner starting at 33–1.

Factors 1, 2 and 3 – definite positives in the profile – are basic qualifications that characterise the typical winner of the great race. These rules will indicate a long list of possibles from which the eventual winner should come.

However, one can be even more precise in defining the profile, for there are a number of negatives, as well as one other positive, which though not as important as the factors already discussed, nevertheless have considerable significance when it comes to trying to single out the horse or horses with the best prospects. These factors may be regarded as tie-breakers. They are:

1   **Positive tie-breaker – Cheltenham Gold Cup**
    Regardless of what else they have achieved in the current season, horses which ran second down to eighth in the Gold Cup are quality horses which have the class to win a National (the Gold Cup winner hardly ever contests the Aintree race). Two such horses, Minnehoma (7th) and Rough Quest (2nd), have met this qualification in the last 10 years and won the National the same year. All such horses from chasing's Blue Riband should be awarded a

positive as a tie-breaker (PT).

Note that horses which are tailed off in National Hunt races but which, often down to a walk, pass the post, are awarded a placing in the official Form Book. They should be ignored. Only animals that occupied places two to eight in the Gold Cup, and finished with the field, qualify for this positive tie-breaker.

2   Negative tie-breaker – novices this season or last

Eliminate any horse which has competed in a chase for novices during the current season or the previous one.

Jumping is the name of the game in the Grand National, and for all horses it is jumping against seasoned performers that improves their jumping skills. Any horse that lacks at least a season's experience of chasing outside novice class seldom gets around in the Aintree race, let alone wins. Similarly, horses which were novices last year, though not completely without a chance, are suspect propositions.

3   Negative tie-breaker – non-finishers in the current season

Eliminate any horse that has failed to complete the course in a chase more than once in the current season.

A tendency to fall is a hopeless characteristic for an Aintree horse. This rule will not put you off every faller in the actual race, but it will indicate those who are unlikely to get as far as the finish. Statistics over many years support this factor as an eliminator of horses that are unlikely to complete the course.

With National Hunt racing taking place 12 months of the year nowadays, it is sometimes difficult to differentiate between this season and last. The break between the two seasons in a horse's form figures given in the press is indicated by a hyphen, for example 3-342P5. For practical purposes, readers should follow that indicator when applying this negative tie-breaker.

4   **Negative tie-breaker – too many outings this season**
Eliminate any horse that has run more than six times in the current season.

No horse can realistically be expected to win the great race if it has had its energy reserves depleted by too much racing. This rule too is well supported by statistics over many years, at least as far as modern renewals of the race are concerned.

5   **Negative tie-breaker – yet to win three chases**
The logic here is similar to that behind tie-breaker 2, and even more potent as an indicator of a horse lacking the necessary credentials to win. In the last 10 years there have been 44 National horses, representing 12 per cent of the total fields, which have not won at least three times over fences. Not one has won, and only two placed. Strangely enough, it is often possible to eliminate even well-backed runners using this tie-breaker, perhaps the single most important of the negatives which can be used to weed out weak canditates from the list indicated by the three positives.

Four positives in all and four negatives (five if novices this season are separated from last) set a very high standard for any race. The Grand National field is fixed at a maximum of 40 runners. It might surprise some readers that even one horse could pass such a set of fairly rigorous tests despite this size of field. Yet this is far from being the case, as an analysis of this year's race will demonstrate. The complete profile for all the runners is given on the next page. Since the process of assigning positives and negatives is quite a complex one, readers are recommended to lay out their own future analyses in a similar fashion. As can be seen from the column on the left, this method has the advantage of producing a positive/negative score for each horse.

With the chart complete, the three main positives should be examined to produce a long list of possible candidates to win the race, before negative factors are considered.

The fourth positive, the tie-breaker from the Cheltenham Gold Cup, did not throw up a qualifier this year and could be ignored. If there had been a horse to list, it could have been awarded its 'PT' to offset a 'P' lacking in the left-hand column, or perhaps to enhance three 'P's already there, which would have made the horse something of a banker.

The actual long list for the race (horses with three 'P's) would have been as follows:

> BINDAREE
> SOUTHERN STAR
> HEDGEHUNTER
> SHARDAM
> JOSS NAYLOR
> AMBERLEIGH HOUSE
> JURANCON II
> CLAN ROYAL
> BEAR ON BOARD

Any one of these horses was capable of winning the race, having scored positives for the three most important factors. For practical purposes, however, it would have been necessary to reduce the nine horses by next examining the negative tie-breakers. When this is done, a clearer picture becomes possible.

GRAND NATIONAL – POSITIVES AND NEGATIVES

RUNNERS POSITIVE (P) 11–5 TO 9–8

Runner	
Le Coudray 11–12	P
Monty's Pass 11–10	P
What's Up Boys 11–9	P
Alexander Banquet 11–8	
Kingsmark 11–7	
Artic Jack 11–7	P
Risk Accessor 11–4	P
David's Lad 11–4	P, P
Bindaree 11–4	P, P, P
Alcapone 11–0	P
Puntal 10–13	P, NT, NT
Southern Star 10–13	P, P, P
Hedgehunter 10–12	P, P, P, NT, NT
Shardam 10–11	P, P, P, NT, NT
Takagi 10–11	P, P
Joss Naylor 10–11	P, P, P, NT
Amberleigh House 10–10	P, P, P
The Bunny Boiler 10–8	P
Tyneandthyneagain (non-runner)	
Gunner Welburn 10–8	P, P, NT
Kelami 10–7	P, NT
Jurancon II 10–7	P, P, P, NT
Royal Atalza 10–6	P, NT
Just In Debt 10–5	P, NT, NT
Exit To Wave 10–5	P
Clan Royal 10–5	P, P, P
Akarus 10–4	P, P, NT, NT, NT
Spot The Difference 10–4	P, P
Bounce Back 10–4	P, P, NT
Ardent Scout 10–3	P, P
Bear On Board 10–1 (9–12)	P, P, P, NT
Lord Atterbury 10–1 (9–12)	P, NT
Mantles Prince 10–1 (9–12)	P, NT
Blowing Wind 10–1 (9–12)	P
Skycab 10–1 (9–11)	P
Wonder Weasel 10–0 (9–7)	P, NT, NT
Smarty 10–0 (9–7)	
Montreal 10–0 (9–0)	NT, NT
Luzcadou 10–0 (9–2)	NT, NT
Bramblehill Duke 10–0 (8–12)	NT, NT

POSITIVE (P) 1, 2, 3 – 3m 2f+

Akarus
Amberleigh House
Ardent Scout
Artic Jack
Bear On Board
Bindaree
Bounce Back
Clan Royal
Hedgehunter
Joss Naylor
Jurancon II
Shardam
Southern Star
Spot The Difference
Tyneandthyneagain
WonderWeasel

POSITIVE (P) 28–1 or less

Amberleigh House 16–1
Bear On Board 14–1
Bindaree 12–1
Clan Royal 12–1
David's Lad 12–1
Gunner Welburn 22–1
Hedgehunter 12–1
Joss Naylor 10–1
Jurancon II 10–1
Le Coudray 25–1
Monty's Pass 18–1
Shardam 18–1
Southern Star 22–1
Takagi 18–1
What's Up Boys 25–1

POSITIVE TIE-BREAKER (PT) 2-8 Cheltenham Gold Cup

No qualifier

NEGATIVE TIE-BREAKER (NT) Novice this season

No qualifier

NEGATIVE TIE-BREAKER (NT) Novice last season

Akarus
Bear On Board
Hedgehunter
Joss Naylor
Jurancon II
Lord Atterbury
Montreal
Puntal

NEGATIVE TIE-BREAKER (NT) Failed to complete twice this season

Akarus
Bramblehill Duke
Gunner Welburn
Luzcadou
Montreal
Shardam
Tyneandthyneagain
Wonder Weasel

NEGATIVE TIE-BREAKER (NT) More than six outings this season

Bramblehill Duke
Just In Debt
Luzacadou
Puntal
Shardam
TyneandThyneAgain
Wonder Weasel

NEGATIVE TIE-BREAKER (NT) Yet to win 3 chases

Akarus
Bounce Back
Hedgehunter
Just In Debt
Kelami
Mantles Prince
Royal Atalza
Tyneandthyneagain

BINDAREE	P, P, P
SOUTHERN STAR	P, P, P
HEDGEHUNTER	P, P, P, NT, NT
SHARDAM	P, P, P, NT, NT
JOSS NAYLOR	P, P, P, NT
AMBERLEIGH HOUSE	P, P, P
JURANCON II	P, P, P, NT
CLAN ROYAL	P, P, P
BEAR ON BOARD	P, P, P, NT

Of this long list, Hedgehunter and Shardam would have been the first to go on account of their double negatives. That left seven horses, again rather too many, even for the purposes of framing a multiple bet.

Joss Naylor and Jurancon II were two of several horses disputing favouritism. Both had emerged from novice class this season, as had Bear On Board, although his final appearance in a chase for novices went right back to the beginning of the previous season. Since then he had been competing against fully fledged chasers for the best part of two full seasons.

Should these three horses have been eliminated? Here interpretation had a part to play in applying the profile.

Bear On Board definitely needed soft ground to bring his stamina into play over the marathon trip. The going was good at Aintree on National Day. Bear On Board was also known to lack the speed to make a race of it with quicker types who could also stay. As for Jurancon II, he was only a seven-year-old. The last seven-year-old to win the race was Bogskar in 1940. Jurancon II looked too young and inexperienced for the job.

If these two had been removed from the list, that left Joss Naylor whose single 'NT' might be overlooked, plus the horses with three 'P's and no negatives against them:

BINDAREE (Winner of the National two seasons ago. Still only 10).

SOUTHERN STAR (Made no show in the race last year, obviously hating the Aintree fences).

JOSS NAYLOR (Perhaps lacking in experience, but second in the high-class Hennessy Cognac Gold Cup).

AMBERLEIGH HOUSE (Fine record over the National fences, but now 12 years old).

CLAN ROYAL (Only once out of the first four in 19 races; well-handicapped).

We now know that Amberleigh House won at 16–1, with Clan Royal second at 10–1, and any further analysis here would probably lead to accusations of hindsight. However, the profile had proved its worth. The field had been cut from 40 to just five horses with an outstanding chance of winning. At this point, users of the profile would have had to 'pay their money and take their choice', as the old expression goes, although it would have been possible to construct a group bet on all five horses using the technique explained in Chapter 5 to produce a profit of approximately £190 on a £100 bet, provided the list of five contained the winner.

Remember that horses sometimes fall in the Grand National through no real fault of their own. Even a horse with brilliant credentials may be badly impeded or brought down altogether. In other words, the element of luck can never be eliminated from the race for those who bet on it, and wise speculators will have several horses, not just one, on their side.

However, whether you opt to go for a single selection or a number of horses, the profile explained in this section can prove invaluable in future years. Once in a while a National winner will slip through the net of positives and negatives, but most of the time it will pick out the right horses in the most competitive race of all.

A Plan for Doubles

As we have seen in an earlier chapter, most non-handicaps are won by either the first, second or third favourite. If that is a fact which applies to most races of this type, it certainly applies to any one race, and the chances of the winners of two races taken together coming from this group are only marginally less in statistical terms. This is the germ of a good doubles plan.

The doubles possibilities are as follows:

Race 1	Favourite with	Favourite with	Favourite with
Race 2	Favourite	2nd Favourite	3rd Favourite
Race 1	2nd Favourite with	2nd Favourite with	2nd Favourite with
Race 2	Favourite	2nd Favourite	3rd Favourite
Race 1	3rd Favourite with	3rd Favourite with	3rd Favourite with
Race 2	Favourite	2nd Favourite	3rd Favourite

If favourites win more often than second favourites, which in turn succeed more frequently than third favourites, then the statistical probability must be that certain of the above nine combinations are much more likely to win than others.

In betting terms it is suggested that these combinations offer the best prospects of striking a winning double:

Race 1	Favourite
Race 2	Favourite
Race 1	Favourite
Race 2	2nd Favourite

Race 1	Favourite
Race 2	3rd Favourite
Race 1	2nd Favourite
Race 2	Favourite
Race 1	3rd Favourite
Race 2	Favourite

If the clever backer can pick the right races, there are excellent medium-to-long-term prospects of a sound profit by exploiting the above pattern. The trick is to choose horses at reasonable prices in races where the rest of the field beyond the first three in the market appear to have no chance. There will not be two opportunities every racing day but, for the backer who is prepared to wait for it, every now and then a golden chance will come along.

Take this example:

Race 1	11–8, 2–1, 3–1
Race 2	13–8, 7–2, 5–1

POSSIBLE RETURNS FROM FIVE £1 DOUBLES = £5 STAKED

Odds			Returns	Profit
11–8	and	13–8	£6.26	£1.26
11–8	and	7–2	£10.71	£5.71
11–8	and	5–1	£14.28	£9.28
2–1	and	13–8	£7.89	£2.89
3–1	and	13–8	£10.52	£5.52

Thus with two favourites at just over odds against and the rest of the prices in betting proportion, any winning combination produces a profit of some sort. Inevitably there will be losing races too and these must be accepted as a fact of betting life to be offset against winning days. Over a reasonable betting period, however, the keen form student should be able to pick and choose to the extent that it is highly probable that the market leaders will include the winners of the two races selected. If he/she can also cut out races where there is likely to be an odds-on favourite, a minimum of one winning favourite will nearly always pick up a reasonable gain.

Skill and patience are needed to work this plan but it has statistics on its side, and in the right hands can be a money-spinner. Obviously it can be worked on the Flat or over the jumps.

Flat Handicap Doubles

A similar plan for handicaps concentrates on races with only six or seven runners and a weak favourite. The system bet is the second and third favourites in four doubles. Again skill is needed in the application of the plan, but it is capable of landing doubles of up to 40–1 for only a small outlay. The method seems to work best on the Flat where handicap favourites succeed less often and there are no fallers to spoil the party.

Top Weights Method for the Flat

It is a statistical fact that horses near the top of the weights predominate in two types of Flat handicap, namely races over the minimum trip of five furlongs and in contests of two miles or more. Between these two extremes, winners come from all points in the weight range.

Taking the first four, five or six runners from the top of the handicap depending on the size of the field in five-furlong or two-miles-and-over races, the backer has a small group which ought to include the eventual winner. He/she can then make an informed choice based on form and the betting market. The betting is generally a fair indicator in both types of race which feature specialists running over their best distances. As for form, consistency represented by good win-and-place performances in each of the last three or four runs provides a vital clue about staying animals likely to go close. Sprinters, however, tend to beat one another from race to race, so don't be put off by a form line of indifferent recent runs. The ability to win is important though, and a potential sprint winner should have got its head in front at least once in its last four or five races.

Doubles Plan for Chases

This little plan aims to exploit the high incidence of winning favourites in three-mile chases, both handicaps and non-handicaps, which is a feature of the winter months, particularly in small fields.

The bet is as follows:

3m NON-HANDICAP CHASE – Favourite
3m HANDICAP CHASE – Favourite and 2nd Favourite
Two win doubles

As for earlier plans for doubles, great care must be exercised in the choice of races, and favourites that are likely to start at odds-on in the non-handicap chase should be avoided. But, if two or three good opportunities can be located each week, a decent long-term profit may well accrue from this simple but highly effective method.

Form System for Jumpers

For those who like a spot of arithmetic and are content to rely on an automatic guide to finding winners, the following system has yielded consistent gains over the years.

It has a double form element. First, it singles out a horse which has a good record over the distance of the race, a factor which tends to be discounted over jumps when compared to the prominence it is given in the analysis of Flat form, but which is an important one in National Hunt racing nevertheless. The horse with the best form figures calculated according to a numerical scale becomes a selection if it is also the most prolific winner over the distance.

Qualifiers have the merit of not all starting at very short odds. A good percentage of winners, some at decent prices, produces a seasonal gain that most punters would consider well worthwhile.

Here are the rules of the plan:

1   Bet on all races under National Hunt rules in Britain from the middle of October (say, 15 October) up to and including the last day of the Cheltenham Festival in March the following year.

2   Bet only in non-handicaps. Claiming races are not considered non-handicaps.

3   To qualify, a horse must have won more times over the distance than any other in the race. Wins in bumpers do not count in hurdle races or chases; wins in hurdle races do not count in chases. Only some daily newspapers follow this practice when placing a 'D' next to a horse's name. It is important to find one that does before beginning to work the system. Also, not all newspapers give the number of times a horse has won over the distance. This information is essential for the system. The racecards of the *Daily Mail,* for example, satisfy these requirements on both counts.

4   Assess runners according to the following scale applied to their three latest public outings, but ignore completely all horses which have not had three runs in their career so far.

WIN	–	1 point
SECOND	–	2 points
THIRD	–	3 points
FOURTH	–	4 points
UNPLACED or failed to finish	–	5 points

5   To qualify, a horse must have the lowest form count of all the runners. If two or more horses have the joint lowest form count, none can qualify for a bet.

6   The horse with the clear best form count (i.e. the lowest) must also have recorded the most wins over the distance of the race. Again, ties among distance winners disqualify a horse from becoming a bet.

7   A qualifier must be running within 50 days of its last public outing.

This is the complete system record for the 2003–2004 National Hunt season. Non-runners have not been included:

FORM HORSES (best form-figure count/most distance wins) over Jumps, 15 October 2003 – 18 March 2004
Stake: £10 each qualifier

			Profit (+) or Loss (–)	Total Profit (+) or Loss (–)
23/10/03	RIVAL BIDDER	Won 4–7	+£5.71	+£5.71
24/10/03	BROTHER JOE	Won 40–85	+£4.71	+£10.42
25/10/03	PHARPOST	Won 10–11	+£9.09	+£19.51
28/10/03	OLLIE MAGEM	Won 7–4	+£17.50	+£37.01
29/10/03	MANTILLA	Won 14–1	+£140.00	+£177.01
02/11/03	MULTEEN RIVER	Won 11–10	+£11.00	+£188.01
08/11/03	CHAMPAGNE HARRY	Won 6–1	+£60.00	+£248.01
08/11/03	BROTHER JOE	Won 11–10	+£11.00	+£259.01
15/11/03	WEB PERCEPTIONS	Lost	–£10.00	+£249.01

			Profit (+) or Loss (−)	Total Profit (+) or Loss (−)
16/11/03	PROVOCATIVE	Lost	−£10.00	+£239.01
22/11/03	WEB PERCEPTIONS	Lost	−£10.00	+£229.01
22/11/03	SANTENAY	Won 13–8	+£16.25	+£245.26
23/11/03	TIRLEY STORM	Lost	−£10.00	+£235.26
25/11/03	LOOK COLLONGES	Lost	−£10.00	+£225.26
26/11/03	BUSH PARK	Won 8–1	+£80.00	+£305.26
27/11/03	OVERSTRAND	Won 1–2	+£5.00	+£310.26
29/11/03	ALBUHERA	Won 7–4	+£17.50	+£327.76
29/11/03	PUNTAL	Won 30–100	+£3.00	+£330.76
30/11/03	MISTY FUTURE	Lost	−£10.00	+£320.76
30/11/03	BALLYCASSIDY	Won 2–1	+£20.00	+£340.76
01/12/03	DEMPSEY	Won 2–11	+£1.82	+£342.58
04/12/03	ISLAND STREAM	Lost	−£10.00	+£332.58
05/12/03	CHICUELO	Lost	−£10.00	+£322.58
06/12/03	OUR ARMAGEDDON	Won 6–4	+£15.00	+£337.58
10/12/03	SO SURE	Lost	−£10.00	+£327.58
10/12/03	BALLYCASSIDY	Won 1–8	+£1.25	+£328.83
12/12/03	STROMNESS	Won 1–14	+£0.71	+£329.54
12/12/03	GREY REPORT	Won 4–5	+£8.00	+£337.54
13/12/03	KINGSMARK	Lost	−£10.00	+£327.54
17/12/03	ARCHIE BABE	Lost	−£10.00	+£317.54
19/12/03	BARACOUDA	Won 2–7	+£2.86	+£320.40
19/12/03	ALBUHERA	Lost	−£10.00	+£310.40
26/12/03	PROVOCATIVE	Won 2–1	+£20.00	+£330.40
26/12/03	BALLYCASSIDY	Lost	−£10.00	+£320.40
26/12/03	COUNTESS CAMILLA	Lost	−£10.00	+£310.40
26/12/03	HENRIETTA	Lost	−£10.00	+£300.40
27/12/03	THISTHATANDTOTHER	Lost	−£10.00	+£290.40
01/01/04	TROUBLE AT BAY	Won 5–6	+£8.33	+£298.73
08/01/04	KERCABELLEC	Lost	−£10.00	+£288.73
09/01/04	GREGORIAN	Won 11–10	+£11.00	+£299.73
09/01/04	BONUS BRIDGE	Won 9–1	+£90.00	+£389.73
12/01/04	THE GREY BUTLER	Lost	−£10.00	+£379.73
13/01/04	OPTIMAITE	Lost	−£10.00	+£369.73
14/01/04	CHIEF YEOMAN	Won 13–2	+£65.00	+£434.73
17/01/04	LORD SAM	Won 4–11	+£3.64	+£438.37
17/01/04	CARACCIOLA	Lost	−£10.00	+£428.37
19/01/04	SALHOOD	Won 6–4	+£15.00	+£443.37
19/01/04	THE BANDIT	Won 5–4	+£12.50	+£455.87
27/01/04	LALAGUNE	Lost	−£10.00	+£445.87
31/01/04	BONUS BRIDGE	Lost	−£10.00	+£435.87
31/01/04	CONTRABAND	Lost	−£10.00	+£425.87
02/02/04	ROSSLEA	Won 10–11	+£9.09	+£434.96
02/02/04	OVERSTRAND	Lost	−£10.00	+£424.96

			Profit (+) or Loss (–)	Total Profit (+) or Loss (–)
10/02/04	BRAMLYNN BROOK	Lost	–£10.00	+£414.96
12/02/04	EDREDON BLEU	Won 1–5	+£2.00	+£416.96
14/02/04	KADARANN	Lost	–£10.00	+£406.96
14/02/04	KING REVO	Won 6–5	+£12.00	+£418.96
20/02/04	RUSSIAN GIGOLO	Lost	–£10.00	+£408.96
21/02/04	BOURBON MANHATTAN	Lost	–£10.00	+£398.96
22/02/04	TIGHTEN YOUR BELT	Won 4–6	+£6.67	+£405.63
23/02/04	JOE'S EDGE	Won 5–4	+£12.50	+£418.13
24/02/04	MOBASHER	Lost	–£10.00	+£408.13
05/03/04	GREY REPORT	Lost	–£10.00	+£398.13
11/03/04	RUM POINTER	Won 30–100	+£3.00	+£401.13
18/03/04	TROUBLE AT BAY	Lost	–£10.00	+£391.13
18/03/04	BARACOUDA	Lost	–£10.00	+£381.13

Total number of bets: 66
Number of winners: 34
Number of losers: 32
Percentage of winners: 51.5
Profit: £381.13
Outlay: £660.00
Percentage of profit on outlay: 57.8

There is no certainty of course that similar success rates can be achieved in future seasons, but with winners in a slight majority over losers in this example season, it is hard to see how a user of the system can come to much harm, even though the percentages may not be maintained in years to come. Equally, there is absolutely no reason why the plan should not do as well again as previously.

The Four-Day Plan over Jumps

In recent years a number of racing journalists concerned with systematic betting, rather than the study of form without fixed rules of selection, have chronicled what has become known as the 'Four-Day Plan' as an automatic road to profit.

The idea is simple enough. Any horse which won its last race and is reappearing in another race within one, two, three or four days qualifies for a bet. The reasoning behind the concept is also straightforward. Winners judged fit and well enough to come out and run again within a very short time, without the customary rest period, must have an excellent chance of following up if their trainers are confident that they have held their form. Thus the aim is to strike while the iron is hot both for connections and the system worker.

Despite the praise which has been showered on the Four-Day Plan, however, results are in fact extremely variable. On the Flat there are a lot more selections than the newcomer to the method might realise. Winners average about one in four and that means there are a great many losers for the punter to contend with. The plan is dependent for long-term gain on horses which start at reasonably good, but not long odds, for the most part. In some seasons a small profit in the region of 10 to 20 per cent is the very best that can be hoped for, while in other years a small overall deficit accrues.

This is obviously a case of so near and yet so far. Consquently there have been many attempts to tweak the basic plan in the hope of boosting the gains to a more acceptable level. Extending the time lapse allowed to five days, betting only in handicaps, omitting qualifiers due to run at the most competitive meetings featuring top-class racing, linking qualifiers to a high rating in a private handicap, all these and other ideas, either singly or in combination, have been tried. Adherents of one combination of factors or another often swear by their own unique method, but this writer has to say that, despite a great deal of experiment, he has never found a way of converting what is without doubt a sound betting angle into a real money-spinner on the Flat.

At the all-weather meetings the same basic four-day concept does better in percentage terms. About one in three qualifiers wins, but everyone seems aware of the potential of these horses, and starting prices are mostly on the low side. The follower of the method on sand can expect consistent losses long term which would be almost impossible to turn into a worthwhile gain.

What of National Hunt racing? Here the picture is much more attractive, provided it is accepted that winter jump racing falls naturally into two halves. Up to the end of the year, from about the middle of October onwards, when the summer jumpers have left the scene, jump racing proper holds centre stage, but the really classy animals aiming for the big prizes in the lead-up to Cheltenham and at the Festival itself, do not appear in force until around Christmas or into the New Year. With them there is no question of exploiting superior fitness and a form peak to bag an extra prize while the time is right for some pot-hunting. Their build-up to top form is much more gradual, and they are given plenty of time to recover from their exertions after a race.

It is otherwise in the last months of the year. Then some jumpers, with no long-term pretensions to the better prizes, are brought out quickly after a win if they have not had a hard race and prospects seem good for a repeat. There are not many of them each season but they are there, and the alert backer can make money from them.

Our four-day scheme is extremely unsophisticated therefore but, like so many successful plans, it wins because it relates a certain type of horse to conditions prevailing at a given time of year which are favourable to it.

From 15 October (an arbitrary date in the month, but some working rule for the system operator is necessary) to 31 December, back any jumper which won its last race and is reappearing on the racecourse within four days of that winning run. This information is shown in all newspapers where the 'days since last outing' is now a standard feature of every modern racecard. There is no tedious checking in form books therefore, and qualifiers can be found in a matter of a very few minutes.

Here is the system record for a very recent period:

FOUR-DAY WINNERS OVER JUMPS
(15 October 2003 – 31 December 2003)
Stake: £10 each qualifier

			Profit (+) or Loss (–)	Total Profit (+) or Loss (–)
18/10/03	BOLTON BARRIE	Lost	–£10.00	–£10.00
24/10/03	ARAGLIN	Lost	–£10.00	–£20.00
29/10/03	PENTHOUSE MINSTREL	Won 8–1	+£80.00	+£60.00
29/10/03	PHARPOST	Lost	–£10.00	+£50.00
01/11/03	ALBUHERA	Lost	–£10.00	+£40.00
03/11/03	MY SHARP GREY	Lost	–£10.00	+£30.00
14/11/03	WATER SPORTS	Won 8–13	+£6.15	+£36.15
15/11/03	INTERDIT	Won 11–10	+£11.00	+£47.15
19/11/03	DUKE OF BUCKINGHAM	Won 11–4	+£27.50	+£74.65
19/11/03	CARAPUCE	Won 4–6	+£6.67	+£81.32
20/11/03	MINSTER GLORY	Won 8–13	+£6.15	+£87.47
21/11/03	MUMBLING	Lost	–£10.00	+£77.47
24/11/03	LORD OF THE HILL	Won 5–2	+£25.00	+£102.47
25/11/03	PHAR FROM FROSTY	Won 1–3	+£3.33	+£105.80
01/12/03	STAR TROOPER	Lost	–£10.00	+£95.80
01/12/03	BELL LANE LAD	Lost	–£10.00	+£85.80
05/12/03	INTENSITY	Won 4–1	+£40.00	+£125.80
12/12/03	PEROUSE	Won 9–4	+£22.50	+£148.30
31/12/03	MAGICAL BAILIWICK	Won 9–2	+£45.00	+£193.30

So there were 19 qualifiers during the period of betting laid down by the system. Of these, 11 won to yield a winning percentage of 57.9. The profit on an outlay of £190 at £10 level stakes was 101.7 per cent.

For readers of this book who are prepared to risk a few pounds on a sound horse racing investment, the Four-Day Plan used at a certain point in the National Hunt season could be 'a nice little earner', to use a modern phrase much in vogue. Even if things go wrong, and the expected profit does not materialise, it is highly unlikely that the whole or even most of the outlay would be lost. The plan gives a distinct 'edge' over the bookmaker, and this edge can be exploited by backers just as some trainers are happy to exploit the same edge in a different way to increase their stables' earnings.

Saturday's Big Chase in Early Winter

Saturday's big chase, usually a handicap, is the highlight of the racing week during the rather flat period between the opening of the National Hunt season 'proper' in October and the Christmas break. To this close observer of the jumping scene, it had always seemed that these races regularly produce a number of winning favourites which, because of the competitiveness of events of their kind, are returned at better-than-average starting prices. Some years ago a little research confirmed that there were indeed quite a few successful market leaders most years in the big handicap chase on Saturdays in the months of October, November and December, but not during January and after, probably because the new year brings very heavy going and form upsets. Although not as many as one would like, there are in fact enough winning favourites at good prices in the pre-Christmas period to make a straightforward bet on the favourite a sporting proposition.

Below is the record of this simple idea over three recent seasons. Year 3 is the most recent. Stakes were calculated this time to a 'pony' (£25), and all bets were at level stakes on the unnamed favourite, not a named horse indicated by a newspaper betting forecast. Where there was any doubt as to which race constituted the most important handicap chase on a Saturday, it was the one which had the highest penalty value to the winner that became the system race. This figure is shown in brackets after the added money following the race title on racecards in all newspapers. Readers who operate the plan in the future are likewise recommended to use this penalty-value figure in cases of doubt.

RECORD OF FAVOURITES IN SATURDAY'S MOST VALUABLE HANDICAP CHASE (October–December)
Stake: £25 each qualifier

Year 1

		Favourite	Profit (+) or Loss (–)	Total Profit (+) or Loss (–)
6 October	1.30 Chepstow	Won 15–8	+£46.88	+£46.88
13 October	4.30 Bangor	Won 11–4	+£68.75	+£115.63
20 October	3.20 Market Rasen	2nd 5–4	–£25.00	+£90.63
27 October	3.25 Kempton	2nd 9–4	–£25.00	+£65.63
3 November	2.35 Ascot	2nd 9–2	–£25.00	+£40.63
10 November	3.15 Wincanton	Won 11–4	+£68.75	+£109.38
17 November	2.50 Cheltenham	Won 9–4	+£56.25	+£165.63
24 November	2.30 Ascot	2nd 8–13	–£25.00	+£140.63
1 December	2.20 Newbury	Unplaced	–£25.00	+£115.63
8 December	1.40 Wetherby	4th 100–30	–£25.00	+£90.63
15 December	1.40 Doncaster	2nd 9–4	–£25.00	+£65.63
22 December	2.00 Ascot	Won 5–2	+£62.50	+£128.13
29 December	2.15 Newbury	3rd 4–1	–£25.00	+£103.13

Year 2

		Favourite	Profit (+) or Loss (–)	Total Profit (+) or Loss (–)
5 October	3.30 Chepstow	4th 100–30	–£25.00	–£25.00
12 October	3.20 Bangor	Unplaced	–£25.00	–£50.00
19 October	3.35 Stratford	Won 9–4	+£56.25	+£6.25
26 October	4.10 Kempton	Won 7–2	+£87.50	+£93.75
2 November	2.20 Ascot	Won 15–8	+£46.88	+£140.63
9 November	2.40 Wincanton	3rd 100–30	–£25.00	+£115.63
16 November	2.50 Cheltenham	Unplaced	–£25.00	+£90.63
23 November	2.35 Aintree	Unplaced	–£25.00	+£65.63
30 November	2.35 Newbury	Unplaced	–£25.00	+£40.63
7 December	2.20 Chepstow	Won 2–1jt	+£12.50	+£53.13
14 December	2.30 Cheltenham	4th 100–30	–£25.00	+£28.13
21 December	1.50 Ascot	Unplaced	–£25.00	+£3.13
28 December	2.15 Musselburgh	4th 3–1	–£25.00	–£21.87

Year 3

		Favourite	Profit (+) or Loss (−)	Total Profit (+) or Loss (−)
4 October	3.30 Chepstow	Unplaced	−£25.00	−£25.00
11 October	2.25 Bangor	Won 5–1	+£125.00	+£100.00
18 October	3.35 Market Rasen	Won 8–11	+£18.18	+£118.18
25 October	3.35 Kempton	Won 100–30	+£83.33	+£201.51
1 November	2.15 Ascot	Unplaced	−£25.00	+£176.51
8 November	2.15 Wincanton	Won 2–1	+£50.00	+£226.51
15 November	2.45 Cheltenham	Won 3–1	+£75.00	+£301.51
22 November	2.10 Ascot	3rd 9–4	−£25.00	+£276.51
29 November	2.35 Newbury	Won 5–1jt	+£50.00	+£326.51
6 December	2.10 Chepstow	Unplaced	−£25.00	+£301.51
13 December	2.30 Cheltenham	Unplaced	−£25.00	+£276.51
20 December	1.15 Ascot	Unplaced	−£25.00	+£251.51
27 December	2.15 Chepstow	2nd 2–1	−£25.00	+£226.51

Results were on the whole favourable therefore. Year 1 showed a profit which may be regarded as acceptable, given the shortness of the sequence of bets. Year 2 recorded a tiny loss unfortunately, but in Year 3 the plan redeemed itself with a worthwhile reward from some lively betting that gives the backer an interest in many of the most important races during the period under review. The six winners from 13 races yielded a profit on outlay of £226.51 or 69.7 per cent.

Despite the variability in performance from season to season, this plan has been included in these pages not only because it offers a very real prospect of a fair gain for readers, but also because its record suggests that even in a bad year when the expected profit proves elusive, it is unlikely that the backer could lose very much. Year 2, for example, was a poor one which produced only three clear winning favourites and one successful joint favourite, a strike rate some way below the statistical average for favourites in all races. Yet the sequence ended with a deficit of less than one point overall. Moreover, there is enough evidence in the three years examined to suggest that a whitewash or near-whitewash, though not impossible, is unlikely in the extreme. Looking even more on the bright side, the three-year analysis of results should convince all but the most pessimistic that the idea could well be profitable in the seasons ahead.

Conclusions

It will have become apparent by now that the kind of formulae explained in this chapter will for the most part only produce marginal profits on outlay. Anyone looking for a huge capital gain from their racing using comparatively small stakes should look to the chapters earlier in this book where multiple bets which roll up profits from a plural number of winners on the accumulator principle are discussed. Given a great deal of luck, these alone can produce a really big profit in a single coup.

However, it is hoped the foregoing pages will have demonstrated that racing systems can be made to pay. There is considerable variety in the type of system discussed, but all those which have been recommended go some way towards eliminating random choice and haphazard results from the hazardous enterprise of trying to conjure regular profits from backing horses.

There are a number of features which characterise a good racing system. In the first place it should be based on sound logic that preferably gives its users some angle or 'edge' to exploit, which will put them ahead of other punters and at an advantage over the bookmaker. Many systems work because they are closely linked to conditions that prevail at a given time of year, and this may provide the edge which is needed to produce an overall profit. Leaving aside this chapter's 'automatic' systems with hard-and-fast rules, even general methodologies like 'Form Horses in Late Summer and Early Autumn', 'A Plan for Doubles', the 'Top Weights Method for the Flat', or the 'Doubles Plan for Chases', all require their operator to take into account changing circumstances as either the Flat or jumping season moves from one phase to the next.

Finally, the hallmark of a really sound racing system is that even when things go wrong in the long term, the backer is not too much out of pocket as a result. All the plans in this chapter, except the special formulae for a single race like the Derby or the Grand National, protect the operator from serious loss, barring a totally freak set of results. Even with the Derby or National, the formulae may well meet the standard if viewed over a number of seasons, not just one.

However, it must be admitted that racing systems, the best of them included, do have drawbacks. For instance, almost all of them tend to be variable in the returns they produce. Bets on a short series of races or restricted to a limited period of operation, systems like Royal Ascot handicappers, the Cheltenham plans, or the favourites in Saturday's big chase for example, have this weakness which makes them vulnerable to the losing run. But systems that operate over much longer periods and involving more selections can produce variable returns too. Several good years for a plan may be followed by a bad one. This is not necessarily a reason to write it off immediately. The swings in the overall return, when they do occur, are part of the general unpredictability of the sport of horse racing. The element of gambling can never be eradicated completely from the practice of betting on horses, with or without a system. Anyone who adopts one or more of the systems in this chapter, while approaching their betting in a spirit of optimism, must be prepared for the unexpected outcome in which the expected profit turns out to be a loss. Even the freak return at the end of a period of betting – a complete whitewash on a short series of bets or a really substantial deficit on a more prolonged sequence – cannot be discounted entirely.

There is another point. The passage of time may bring

a change in the conditions that helped a system to succeed in the first place, and may cancel out its edge to a greater or lesser degree. The rules of racing may be altered for a certain type of race. Changes in the Racing Calendar can alter established patterns of form or statistics, which in turn could produce a minor, or even major, upheaval in results. New trainers come along who do things differently from the old ones. Something so apparently innocuous as a change of fashion in breeding, training or riding styles, if relevant to the success of a system, can turn it from a winner into a loser. One bad year is certainly not grounds in itself to dispense with a winning method, but the system worker must be constantly vigilant in watching out for any changes that affect the profitability of a plan.

For those who do not use systems, the business of making racing and betting pay depends on flair and judgement. Automatic racing systems can be dangerous in the wrong hands for, whatever the past and present portents, they can never be absolutely relied upon to deliver the goods. But then nor can flair and judgement, and there is no doubt that the regime of following some organised system of betting can help many punters to chart their way through the betting minefield. There is room therefore for both approaches. This chapter will obviously be of most interest to systemites. It is hoped that they will use the knowledge gained from it wisely and well.

8

Twelve Golden Rules of Successful Betting

1. Always Read Your Bookmaker's Rules

Every bookmaker, whether one of the high street giants or the small, independent operator around the corner, has a set of rules which governs all their transactions with their clients.

If you already patronise one layer and have not been through his 'book of words' with a fine-tooth comb, remedy the defect at once. Equally, if starting to invest with a new firm, at least check how the type of bets you favour will be settled *before* having a bet. This applies particularly to punters who like to bet win and place, or who indulge in fancy conditional bets with, for example, elements of 'any-to-come' or 'stop-at-a-win'.

Also, many readers may not be aware that there is no such thing as a genuine 'no limit' bookmaker in Britain. Even the big national chains will not pay out more than a certain sum on any one day, although it is a pretty astronomical one. As for the 'independents', they have much lower limits. Those who like to bet on multiple wagers involving accumulators on horses at long odds should take particular note. Calculate roughly the possible return in the event of a huge, cumulative bet coming up. Will it go over your bookmaker's limit? There is no point in 'winning' a London town house if it turns out your bookmaker will only pay for a semi-detached in the sticks.

2. If You Bet At Odds-On, Back The Horse Not The Price

'Never bet at odds-on' is definitely bad advice. What is the difference between 10–11 and Evens? Only one of degree, that's all. On the other hand, consistently trying to 'buy money' with odds-on chances for no other reason than they are odds-on is asking for trouble. Too many get beaten, a lot more than people realise.

But there is another consideration. A number of major statistical surveys, taking in results of whole seasons, have demonstrated quite unequivocally that *random* betting on short-priced animals will always yield a better result for the punter than regularly backing horses at longer odds, and the shorter the odds of fancied horses, the more this is so.

There is nothing wrong with laying the odds therefore, but what is more important is that you genuinely fancy the horse, not just its price which makes it look a good thing. The racecourse test frequently reveals that it was anything but a certain winner.

3. Keep Each-Way Bets To A Minimum

The place element of an each-way bet favours the bookmaker, not the backer. This is demonstrated by the table below which shows the true mathematical odds for each of the four standard categories of each-way wager when compared with the bookmaker's price. The theoretical assumption behind the calculations is that every horse has a mathematically equal chance, and the minimum allowable number of runners in each category is taken, as here the backer has the best theoretical chance.

MATHEMATICAL ODDS FOR EACH-WAY BETS
ON REPRESENTATIVE RACES

Race and Odds	True Place Odds	Bookmaker's Price	Advantage to Bookmaker
5 runners	3 against 2	¼ of 4–1	
¼ the odds	or	or	+0.50–1
on 1st and 2nd	1.50–1	Evens	
8 runners	5 against 3	⅕ of 7–1	
⅕ the odds	or	or	+0.27–1
on 1st, 2nd and 3rd	1.67–1	1.40–1	
12 runners	9 against 3	¼ of 11–1	
(Handicaps only)	or	or	+0.25–1
¼ the odds	3–1	2.75–1	
on 1st, 2nd or 3rd			
16 runners	12 against 4	¼ of 15–1	
(Handicaps only)	or	or	−0.75–1
¼ the odds	3–1	3.75–1	
on 1st, 2nd, 3rd and 4th			

So only in the last category where backers have 12 horses against them and four for them, are the place odds in their favour. The true place odds are 12 ÷ 4 or 3–1, but the bookmaker will pay a quarter of 15–1, the true mathematical chance of the backer finding the winner, that is 15 ÷ 4 or 3.75–1 for a place.

Even this is something of an illusion, however. As was shown on pages 13–14, the over-round in handicaps with very big fields is invariably much higher than elsewhere. The bookmaker is able to conceal his high percentage 'take' on the totality of the field because he can chalk up most of the runners at apparently big prices which, in reality, are far less generous than they look.

Therefore only bet each-way sparingly. If you particularly fancy the chances of a horse and wish to insure yourself against a near miss, that is one thing. But betting each-way as a matter of policy on all or most selections will put money in the bookmaker's pocket in the long run.

4. Back Fancied Horses With A Bookmaker, Outsiders On The Tote

An arbitrary rule but a good one is never to back a horse on the Tote which is priced at 9–1 or less by the bookies. The Tote price will rarely beat that set by the bookmakers and, when it comes to favourites, virtually never. But the reverse is very much the case with winners at 10–1 plus, especially in very big fields.

Most people know all this, but few seem willing to change their habitual betting medium to fit circumstances.

However, there are exceptions to the rule of backing fancied horses with the bookmakers, and outsiders on the Tote. Well-backed horses, other than favourites, ridden by an apprentice, an unfashionable jockey, or a lady rider in a race for both sexes, may well pay a better-than-expected Tote dividend. This applies also to horses from very small stables. French-trained runners, but not those from Ireland, are generally best on the Tote unless very near to the head of the market.

Bad value Totalisator bets are horses trained in the elite Newmarket establishments, or ridden by the handful of jockeys at the very top of the tree. Also, horses with good form figures and heavily tipped in the press are poor Tote wagers, as are course specialists whose particular liking for a track is well known to the locals.

Even if your preference is for the 'nanny', the Tote place pool is a mug's game. The Tote's 'take' from the pool is very high, and returns to long-suffering patrons of it paltry.

Of the Tote's speciality bets, the Exacta straight forecast bet is a much better wager than the reversed forecast (first or second in either order) it replaced and which paid laughable returns. Although Tote deductions are still high, there are times when the Exacta can be exploited effectively, especially when a favourite at odds-on or close to it looks vulnerable. Backing the best of the rest to win, with the favourite to come second, can pay some rewarding dividends.

Opinion is divided about the Placepot, where the punter has to find a placed horse in the first six races on the card. The majority of racegoers like to dabble with a small perm before the real action starts, and it is generally regarded as a little insurance that might pay off if the main bets of the day go down.

However, serious backers in the main will have nothing to do with it. The rules in the event of withdrawals one has not backed and for non-runners one has included, though necessary, are just as likely to work against the individual punter as for him or her; and, while it is the same for everybody, tend to make the bet something of a minor lottery. Also, jockeys do not always ride horses out to the finish, whatever they may claim. So in unimportant races it is not always the best horses that actually finish second and third. In addition, the deduction by the Tote is in excess of 25 per cent. However, if you swear by the Placepot as a fun wager with a bit of profit potential, I for one would not attempt to dissuade you from a bet that may enhance your enjoyment of the racing.

The Tote Jackpot, like the Scoop6 on Saturdays, favours syndicates operating big perms, and the lone punter trying to select the winner of six races is up against it. The best time for anyone to have a go at the Jackpot is when there has been a carry-over from a big meeting like Ascot or Cheltenham to a small one. Some of the high rollers may not be paying attention, and the massively swollen pool may be winnable with an inexpensive perm on uncompetitive racing.

5. Do Not Bet 'First Show', Especially On The Racecourse

The first set of prices each bookmaker chalks up on his board are not a serious proposition for the punter. Their object is to test the water and ensure that a layer does not 'catch cold' vis-à-vis his rivals by over-pricing a horse. Because of this, all very early prices are uniformly low, and ridiculously so for the favourite. Prices will lengthen, and only an idiot bets before a proper market has formed.

Satellite prices in the betting shops come later, and their first show is more realistic. Even so it usually pays to wait.

If, on the other hand, it is known that a horse will be the medium of a genuine gamble, then one must get in early before the price shortens. Not many of us are often in this fortunate position, however – fortunate, that is, if the gamble is landed.

6. Treat So-Called 'Information' With The Caution It Deserves

Racing insiders sometimes have access to knowledge which can be of immense value in a betting sense, but for obvious reasons they are not given to telling the world about it.

Talk to enough of the dolly-mixture of ordinary racegoers on the other hand and you can get a tip for every horse on the card. You will probably also get the name of the Derby winner in three years' time, even if it has not yet been foaled!

As for commercial tipsters, forget them. They deal in greed, fantasy and shoddy goods. But, a word from the right quarter that your fancy is fit and well and definitely 'off' today is worth its weight in gold, especially when the 'right quarter' has a definite stable connection.

7. Avoid 'Clues' When Reading Form

Most punters have a favourite indicator which they swear by as an aid to finding winners. Beaten favourites, course and distance winners, top weights in nursery handicaps, the outsider in a three-horse race, horses priced at 9–1, last horse in the betting forecast each-way, first five-year-old from the eight-stone mark downwards in handicaps, most recently placed runner in the field, horses which have travelled over 200 miles to race – these are just a few of the less fanciful.

Many such clues form a part of horse-gambling lore but, although they may pinpoint a winner from time to time, followed consistently over a period they are all certain losers. Racing is just not as simple as that.

8. Following Jockeys' Mounts Is The Road To Ruin

Some people never learn, but if you indulge in this practice long enough, you will go broke in the end. Top jockeys may well be 'the punters' friend' and will often come up with a winner or two, but they also ride a huge percentage of losers (around 80 per cent), and hardly ever show a level-stakes, seasonal profit on all their mounts.

On the other hand, there is a world of difference between betting on a horse for no other reason than that a favourite jockey is riding it, and having extra confidence in an animal selected on other grounds because a top jockey is in the saddle. The jockey factor is important too when a leading rider has been booked by a small stable which does not retain him, especially in a handicap. This is often a powerful hint that a coup is planned. Frankie Dettori will very probably never repeat his 'Magnificent Seven' at Ascot or anywhere else, but a gamble by a clever yard using the services of a crack jockey is a regular part of the racing scene.

If a jockey's mounts followed without discrimination are a highly suspect proposition, the human factor is still as important in racing as the equine. As we saw in an earlier chapter, trainers' methods are well worth close study. Selective betting on runners from the right stable can be a paying game.

9. Keep Accurate Records Of All Bets, And Of All Systems

Probably the worst fault of most backers is their failure to keep detailed, long-term accounts of bets struck. There are very good reasons why record-keeping is so important. In the first place it tells the backer exactly where he or she stands financially. It will give the lie to the fantasy land in which many punters live, where self-delusion convinces them that they are showing a profit or at least breaking about even, when in fact they could be losing, and possibly losing quite heavily. Detailed records bring a healthy dose of reality to punters who in many cases are only too happy to deceive themselves.

However, there is another reason why records of bets are so important. A full betting account will reveal which part of a punter's betting strategy is working and which may not be. Adjustments to established practice can then be made, and stakes perhaps increased on the type of bets that do best. Similarly, losing concepts can be modified or even eliminated altogether.

Record-keeping is even more vital for the person following a system, or monitoring one with a view to perhaps operating it in practice. Not only will this reveal the merits of a plan, but it may show if any part of the rules is a weakness that needs modifying.

Here is one final tip. If you are keeping a record of a system, set down as much detail as possible in your accounts, including information which may not seem directly relevant to the plan in its present form. Sometimes background material which has been recorded may allow the system worker to add in an extra rule or two that makes all the difference between profit and loss. Such a rule, or rules, may only come to light if the ledger shows other factors which might just have a bearing on the system's profitability.

Make no mistake, full and accurate record-keeping is an

absolute necessity for all backers, whether they follow a system or not.

10. Adjust Stakes According To The Time Of The Year

Reduce your Flat stakes drastically or stop betting altogether as soon as the rains come in September or early October. The transition from fast to soft ground plays havoc with form. Also, huge fields are a feature of the autumn on the Flat with so many animals running for their winter corn. There is no point in sacrificing a seasonal profit on the altar of a series of risky bets at this time of the year. Likewise, go very easy on the Flat in March and April. Form has yet to settle down.

With jumpers, form before Christmas is generally overturned afterwards as the better-class animals near their peak, putting early types in the shade. Concentrate on firm ground specialists up to September, but October and November are similar to March and April on the Flat.

11. Don't Bet Just For The Sake Of Betting

Having a bet just for fun and interest is a different matter but, if profit is your main motive, wait for it. The right horses in the right races will come if you have patience.

12. Never, Ever Bet More Than You Can Afford To Lose

This is the golden rule *par excellence* of all gambling, for totally obvious reasons. 'Don't chase your losses' is another racing maxim that should *never* be forgotten.

9

Ten Golden Rules for Gambling on the Betting Exchanges

However popular the betting exchanges may be with those punters (still very much in the minority) who employ their home PC just to try to get a better price about their selection than is available from a conventional bookmaker, a betting exchange is in fact a gambling jungle of a very different kind to the traditional betting scene, and one in which the typical racing enthusiast, for whom this book is written, must proceed with the utmost caution.

The organisers of the exchanges are notoriously uncommunicative about the identity of their clients, but it does appear that the computerised facilities have been hijacked to a great extent by 'traders'; that is, people who are not really interested in betting in the traditional way for pleasure and, hopefully, some profit, but who use an exchange to lay horses to lose as well as back them to win, frequently creating arbitrage situations between several markets from which they can make money whatever the result of a race. The field of combined operations for these professional or semi-professional traders includes not only the regular betting-exchange market on a contest but, when appropriate, the ante-post markets also offered by the exchanges on some races, as well as the odds from conventional bookmakers; and finally, the 'in-running' betting on the exchanges, which gives one of the best opportunities for trading into a 'no-lose', or even a 'green book' position where any bets on a horse make money regardless of whether the horse wins or is beaten.

Traders make tens, perhaps hundreds of bets during a day's racing. Even on one race they might strike a large number of different bets in an effort to maximise gains on some horses and minimise liabilities from others. This is because just a change in the odds of a few decimal points can be turned to advantage, given the necessary mathematical skill and speed of reaction.

The basic trading manoeuvre is to back the same horse at one price, then, if the odds about the horse eventually contract, to lay it to lose at a lower price. Here is the example of basic trading that Betfair, the biggest of the exchanges, gives in its promotional literature.

Suppose you back your selection on the exchange to win at 3.0 (2–1) for a stake of £50. This produces a net profit of £100 plus your £50 stake, a total return of £150 before commission to the exchange.

However, if the price about the horse goes to 2.0 (Evens) as the time of the race approaches, you could lay it to lose for £50 at those odds, with a potential payout of £100.

So, if the horse wins, you have a profit of £50 before commission (£150 minus £50 stake, minus £50 from laying the horse). If the horse loses, you have a deficit of £50 from backing it to win, but you regain this by dint of successfully laying the horse to lose for that amount. Less commission on the lay bet, you break even.

This is the simplest form of trading and, by sophisticated use of the fundamental stratagem of 'backing high and laying low', a skilled trader can build up a whole series of wagers on a race from which he or she has a certain profit, or at the very least has one or more positions in which the odds are much more favourable than would be the case with a straightforward bet on a horse to win or lose. As Betfair adds: 'There are many different scenarios to guarantee profit and some people even bet in-running.'

This is obviously a very different approach to backing

horses from the one which prevailed until the last decade of the twentieth century. There are those who say that this extra dimension to betting on horses is a good thing, whereas others feel that the right to lay horses to lose, without which the trader cannot operate, opens the way to corruption. But be that as it may, what has happened is that in the few short years of their existence the betting exchanges have become more and more like the Stock Exchange futures market on which they are based.

Non-traders, that is those who own a home computer and just like to bet as a pastime, can still use a betting exchange to back horses to win or each-way along the same lines and with the same outcome as in the past. And for the trouble involved in getting their bet matched over the internet they may well be rewarded with better odds. For the typical racing fan who has followed the sport since before the advent of the exchanges, nothing fundamental need change. To such people the result of a race is everything, as it should be for anyone who watches horse racing on television or at the course for entertainment, as well as, more hopefully, some gain.

But the fact remains that most of the betting now done on the exchanges is carried on by a very different breed of speculator. For traders what is vitally important in order to make money is to read the market on any event correctly. 'Tip me the price, not the winner,' is a dictum much quoted in the internet chatrooms included by some of the exchanges as part of their service. Traders' main preoccupation is with *price movements,* with the ancient art of trying to pick the winner of a horse race only a secondary consideration. In this connection, the various competing factions – traders, racing insiders, representatives of conventional bookmakers – are capable of pulling all manner of what might be called 'dodges' in order to gain an advantage over their rivals, and of course over the rest of us who probably only use the exchanges to try to get bigger odds than Tattersall's Ring offers, or can be had by betting at starting price.

As long as the betting exchanges are constituted the way they are, insider dealing and all, traders and other professionals are entitled to do this of course, but in the final analysis it is the ordinary punter who might pay much of the price; for there is only so much money in the punting pot, and the expertise of traders and the like may cream off the lion's share. Mr, Mrs or Miss Average, who begin by looking just for a better price for their selection than can be obtained elsewhere, run the risk of being sucked into something far more difficult, complex and dangerous than was originally intended.

The following rules, therefore, are not a detailed guide to professional trading – a separate book would be needed for that. Rather the Golden Rules given below are there to help the typical racing enthusiast avoid as many as possible of the pitfalls which lie in wait for those who are not entirely familiar with betting exchanges. For readers who are already adept at using the computerised exchanges to back their selection by matching bets with others on the internet, there may be something here they may not have considered which could be of profit to them.

1. Familiarise Yourself With Every Aspect Of The Rules And Procedures Of The Betting Exchange You Are Using

Betting exchanges are a different way of gambling on horses. It is vital to appreciate this. No matter how long you might have followed racing, many preconceived notions applicable to the traditional way of betting will need to be modified to accommodate all the ramifications that follow from the basic matching principle of the exchanges between backer and layer. These, and the opportunities they create for you and others in competition with you, will of necessity alter your perceptions of odds and their value in relation to the sport.

All betting exchanges work in fundamentally the same way, but they differ somewhat in their rules for dealing with a number of the less routine situations that may arise. The biggest exchanges, Betfair and Sporting Options, and the Irish Betdaq, have helplines. Do not be afraid to make use of them if you are uncertain about any point. The exchange will be happy to discuss your problem. Nor will you be alone. The Betfair helpdesk, for instance, dealt with over 4,500 calls during the three days of the most recent Cheltenham Festival.

2. Ante-Post Bets Apart, Be Wary Of Taking Up Offers That Allow You To Back A Horse To Win At Odds Way Above The Prevailing Rate With Conventional Bookmakers, Or Elsewhere In The Exchanges' Markets

When someone on a betting-exchange website offers to lay a horse at well over the price on offer elsewhere, you must ask yourself why, even though in your view the animal in question has a good chance and may be well worth a bet.

One possible explanation for the big price might be that the prospective layer knows something about the horse that is detrimental to its chance, knowledge which is not in the public domain. This is not alarmist. In the relatively short history of the exchanges there have been a number of well-publicised cases which aroused suspicion (to put it mildly), and they may only be the tip of the iceberg.

Racing professionals, some of whom may have very close links with a stable, are not barred from betting on the exchanges, unlike the City where insider dealing is illegal. There is nothing to stop anyone with privileged information about a horse's lack of well-being or fitness, for example, from laying it to lose on an exchange for whatever sum of money they see fit.

By all means try to get the best price you can on the exchange and, if that is above the odds that are available from other sources, then well and good; but unsolicited odds greatly in excess of the going rate may be more a warning sign than a recommendation.

On the other hand, huge odds are regularly on offer in the betting-exchange ante-post markets for the big races in the Calendar, and that includes big stakes events as well as handicaps. Here spectacular prices compared with the bookmakers' odds are so much the norm that there is much less reason for suspicion, although in the 2003–2004 National Hunt season one prominent owner was eventually warned off for six months by the Jockey Club for laying his horse to lose in the ante-post market of an exchange only a day or two before the horse was scratched from an important handicap steeplechase.

However, the following example is much more the rule than the exception where ante-post betting on the exchanges is concerned. The comparisons are for the first four home in the most recent Grand National at the time of writing.

ANTE-POST MARKET ON THE GRAND NATIONAL
February–March 2004

		Highest price on one leading betting exchange		Highest price from one leading ante-post bookmaker
1.	AMBERLEIGH HOUSE	90	(89–1)	25–1
2.	CLAN ROYAL	36	(35–1)	25–1
3.	LORD ATTERBURY	140	(139–1)	33–1
4.	MONTY'S PASS	32	(31–1)	20–1

It is evident, therefore, that the ante-post markets on the exchanges are an exception to the general rule that it is dangerous to match unsolicited offers to lay a horse at an unrealistically high price.

3. When Backing An Outsider, Always Ask For Odds Well In Excess Of The Prevailing Prices With A Conventional Bookmaker Or On The Exchange Itself

If you do not like the odds on offer for your selection, betting exchanges, just like the City markets they imitate, allow the punter the facility of leaving an order on the website for a specified price. This ordering facility should be used to try to obtain the biggest price possible.

Here everything depends on the type of runner you want to back. If your choice is a fancied animal, you are most unlikely to get odds above the going rate on the exchange, but that may not be the case with outsiders. Ask for a big price about your selection and, no matter how fanciful it may seem, there is a chance that someone also using the site will lay the horse at the odds you are asking.

Take as an example Smirfy's Party which won an all-aged, six-furlong handicap at Redcar on 9 August 2003. Smirfy's Party started at 50–1 on the racecourse, but was matched on the Betfair exchange at no less than 340 (339–1)! Someone had obviously decided that the horse had no chance and was willing to pick up what was thought to be some easy money by laying the horse to lose at those odds. Perhaps the stake was not a large one, but the lesson is clear enough.

Prices like the above are matched regularly on the exchanges by people who lay outsiders, looking for a facile profit. This is not in the opinion of this writer the sort of thing readers should indulge in themselves, but they may benefit from that sort of layer and have their selection matched at a big price, *but only if they ask for it*. If the match at the specified odds is not forthcoming, they can always drop their price or, if the worst comes to the worst, take one of the prices currently displayed on the exchange website.

4. Do Not Be Too Rigid In Leaving Orders On The Exchange Site

Betfair claims that on average its odds are some 20 per cent better for fancied horses than those from a bookmaker. Rule 3 recommended backers to ask for a price well above the prevailing rate, certainly when trying to back an outsider. However, by being too rigid in asking for odds well over current rates, it is easy to miss a good bet. Here you are a punter, not a trader. You want only to get the best price you can, and the mathematical manipulations of the trader are no part of your strategy. It would be depressing in the extreme to hold out for, say, 6.0 (5–1) against your selection when it is generally priced at 4.0 (3–1), only to see it romp home at the latter price.

Many of the big-price opportunities on the exchanges crop up when they are least expected. If the punter always expects to be matched at well over the price everyone is taking, this will lead to disappointment, certainly in the case of fancied animals. Given plenty of time before the race is due to be run, the punter can leave an optimistic order, and probably should, but must be prepared to come into line very quickly if these odds are not matched.

However, there are situations when the seasoned backer can exploit the system to get a better price than is currently shown on the screen. Take this classic case:

		BACK	LAY		
14	14.5	15	17.5	18	18.5
£291	£169	£342	£50	£121	£395

Here the spread between the price to back and that to lay is a good opportunity for leaving an order to obtain a price slightly above what is currently available. Leave an order to back the horse at odds of 17 and this will seem to other exchange punters as the best available price to lay and will have excellent prospects of being matched.

Clever tactics apart, however, over-use of the ordering facility born of a constant excess of optimism may be counter-productive in the long run.

5. Laying Horses To Lose Is Not An Automatic Way Of Making Consistent Profits

The most novel aspect of betting exchanges of course is that in every transaction there must be a layer to match the bet struck by the backer. This is much more than a mere innovation in the world of betting. The right of unlicensed persons to lay horses is a truly revolutionary change in the way betting on horses is carried out in this country.

There are those who assert that, given sound judgement, the layer on the exchange has the advantage over the backer, if only because the layer has more horses running for him/her than the backer, and is usually betting at prices below the mathematical odds, in much the same way as conventional bookmakers contrive to do about all the horses in a race with a realistic chance (see page 12 of this book).

However, it would be quite wrong to think that when an unlicensed person lays a horse on an exchange they are acting like a bookmaker, with all the presumed advantages that this implies. Far from having the protection of the over-round to provide an acceptable trading margin on any reasonably balanced 'book', the successful layer must pay a commission to the exchange. The same applies if a number of horses are laid, and it would be impossible for one individual to construct a completely over-round book on an exchange.

The point to realise about laying horses is that just because in pre-exchange days one found it difficult to back winners, this doesn't mean it is easy to pick out losers to lay.

What are you supposed to do? Go through the card each day to find the horse or horses considered to have the best chance of winning, as you used to do, then lay them on an exchange? If the regular pattern of old is repeated for most people, the majority of them will lose and a profit is shown. Such an approach would be a nonsense of course, but there is still a serious point here.

Conversely, a positive approach to seeking out losers must confront the fact that whereas as a backer you give up just a single stake if unsuccessful, as a layer you must pay out at a multiple of the stake according to the odds. Suppose for the sake of argument you lay a series of horses, all at odds of 6.0 (5–1). In order to make a profit on the sequence, you need to be right seven times out of seven. If any horse between the first and fifth in the sequence wins, you will lose overall; and, if the sixth horse wins, you will do no better than break even overall. Do not be fooled. Laying horses is no picnic.

6. Do Not Lay Horses To Lose At Big Odds

The punter who makes a habit of laying outsiders to lose at long odds runs grave risks.

So the punter who laid Hardy Eustace for the Champion Hurdle at 660 (659–1) in February 2004 must have got the shock of his life when the Irish horse outspeeded Rooster Booster to win the hurdling crown at Cheltenham in March. Similarly, the Sussex Stakes at Goodwood in 2003 will be one race a Betfair client will want to forget. He or she laid the eventual winner, Reel Buddy, to lose at 210 (209–1) to a £10 bet in the ante-post market. By comparison Reel Buddy's racecourse starting price was 20–1.

What these examples show of course is that there are no easy pickings on betting exchanges.

7. When Betting In-Running, Your Opinion Is No Worse Than The Next Person's, But No Better

According to Betfair's publicity, one of the most popular of its many markets is 'In-Running' where punters watching a race on TV can back or lay horses using the standard matching principle while it is being run.

This popularity is perfectly understandable. It is very exciting to be able to bet in this way, and be rewarded financially if one's opinion is correct.

Yet such betting is obviously full of danger. Anyone who has watched just a little horse racing will know that the complexion of a race can change very quickly. What seems a sound bet to win one second can look a very poor one only a few seconds later, as horses fade from contention in a few strides, or come bursting through near the finish to win on the post from an apparently hopeless position.

Even the results of jump races, in which the action on the whole takes place much more slowly than on the Flat, can be very hard to predict at different points in a contest. Who can forget Tony McCoy's remarkable ride at Southwell in January 2002 when on Family Business in a novice chase? Family Business fell at the tenth fence leaving four horses still standing in the race. The champion jockey remounted and set off in pursuit about a furlong behind. At this point odds of 1,000 (999–1) were matched on Betfair against him winning. Yet, when the rest of the runners all came down at the remaining fences, Family Business finished alone to win the race. Imagine the feelings of those punters who laid the horse to lose at such ridiculous odds!

Nor are Flat punters immune from such shocks if they indulge in in-running betting. At Lingfield in January 2003, Altay won a one-mile-five-furlong race on the all-weather circuit and was traded at 1.01 (100–1 on) in-running. How did those who had backed the horse at 100–1 on feel when they heard the announcement that it had been disqualified for causing interference on the bend into the straight?

Even without freak results, however, the in-running market really represents nothing more than a hugely risky gamble, given the fact that the view of even a expert race-reader can be proved wrong in a matter of seconds.

As a further caveat to would-be speculators in this market, it is a fact that many punters receive their pictures all of three seconds ahead of others. Those watching terrestial television or SIS have this advantage, but At The Races and Racing UK are subject to the time delay. For those watching the latter, to bet in-running is surely far from ideal.

The only real justification for betting in this way is to try to redeem a bad bet before 'the off' or to complete a trading position. Even then, betting in-running is a big gamble. It is true, however, that some people will happily bet on the progress of flies across a wall if no other betting opportunity is to hand.

8. If You Must Bet In-Running, Avoid Betting At Long Odds-On

As we have seen, the likely result of a horse race can alter so quickly from moment to moment that to bet in-running must always be a risky proposition. However, to an experienced race-reader sometimes one horse stands out from several as the likely winner, even when the field is some way from home. If the probable outcome of a race is absolutely clear-cut, any attempt to back what is judged the certain winner may well not be matched, but if there is even the slightest element of doubt, it might be possible for a backer to have their bet matched at very long odds-on.

This kind of betting is, if anything, even more dangerous than any other sort of in-running gambling, for it allows so little margin of error for the future. Assume someone betting in-running at odds of 1.02 (50–1 on) all the time is right 50 times in a row, and that is a big assumption, but the 51st bet loses, then all the gains so far are immediately wiped out for the backer who has been intent on 'buying money' in this hazardous manner. Anyone who seriously believes they can go on betting and winning in this way continuously is asking for trouble. Yet there are apparently plenty of bettors on the exchanges who seek to make money like this. Sooner or later, it is almost certain that their judgement will err and they must pay out a large sum to a grateful layer who has only risked a relatively tiny amount in stakes.

The example of one day's racing from the 2003 Flat season will show just how easy it is to make a mistake when betting in-running, even though everything appears cut and dried for the backer who thinks they have the winner.

On 9 June, during the running of the Coronation Cup, Highest from the powerful Godolphin stable was matched at 1.01 (100–1 on) to a £2,000 stake on Betfair. Highest finished second.

Later in the afternoon, in the Surrey Stakes over seven furlongs, Naahy traded in-running at 1.02 (50–1 on) for a total of no less than £14,000 on the same exchange. Though Naahy was well clear, in fact four lengths clear of its field at the furlong pole, he was caught close home and beaten a short head by Rimrod in the last stride of the race.

The point about such bets is that for every backer on an exchange, there is a layer. Readers will surely agree with the author that in the case of bets at very long odds-on, it is the layer who has the best of the bargain.

9. Take Nothing At Face Value On The Betting Exchanges And Beware Of Disinformation

Gossip and rumour are inseparable from the sport of horse racing, particularly among those who like to bet on it. 'Information', most of it bad, abounds on the racecourse.

The betting exchanges have brought new significance to this most time-honoured of racing customs. Take the example of the 'corner horse', that is, an animal quoted as an outsider in the morning papers, but which opens up second or third favourite on the course. In the old days, this would have been generally accepted as an indication that the horse had a chance much greater than its bare public form would suggest. In the knowledge that it was a genuine contender, it could be backed with some chance of success. Not any more. Not since the advent of betting exchanges.

Suppose someone well-placed in racing circles begins to circulate a rumour that a horse is in fact much better than its record and is 'expected' by its connections. The animal becomes a corner horse in the racecourse market, but in reality nothing about the rumours of its alleged sound chance of winning is true. All that has happened is that someone wants to lay the horse, in fact a hopeless outsider, on the exchanges. If it had stayed an outsider in the racecourse market, no one would have wanted to back it, not on the course, not on the exchanges, not in the betting shops. But if it is generally accepted as a genuine corner horse, it will attract backers on the exchanges where it can be laid at a false price. In truth it may be a 33–1 chance, and has no prospect of winning, but those taken in by the disinformation may be happy to back it at around, say, 5–1. When the race is run of course, the horse is down the field and someone has made a killing. The unscrupulous rumour-monger will have laid the horse on the exchanges, and will have done so at only 5–1, not 33–1. So if a shock result does occur and the horse wins despite its very slight chance, he or she must pay out at a mere 5–1, not 33–1. But the horse will almost certainly lose, and an animal that would have gone unbacked will have been laid to lose on the exchanges, possibly to not insubstantial sums.

That was an imaginary case, but now the betting exchanges are well established this scenario has become an all-too-common occurence.

Here is a real example of how deliberate disinformation can benefit the unscrupulous punter on the exchanges.

Three weeks before the 2004 Derby at Epsom the Irish colt Yeats was around 4.5 (7–2) on the exchanges and favourite for the big race in their ante-post markets.

Early on the evening of Saturday, 15 May, anyone who switched on their computer and logged on to one of the big exchange sites would have discovered that Yeats had begun to drift in price. The price movement was very gentle at first, but the trend gathered momentum. By about midnight, Yeats was no longer quoted at 4.5, but at 10 points above those odds at 14.5.

Yet by morning, even though the horse had not done a home gallop on Saturday, and no bulletin about its well-being, or lack of it, had been issued by its Ballydoyle stable, Yeats was back to around 4.9 for the Derby, more or less where the odds were on the previous afternoon.

The explanation for this series of events is not hard to find. Almost certainly a person of influence in the betting world had decided to try to fool the market. Well-placed rumours that all was not well with the colt had done the trick. The price of the Derby favourite began to move gradually upwards and what one might call the 'bandwagon effect' had done the rest.

As the odds lengthened, the perpetrators of the coup would have begun to back Yeats for small amounts at the higher prices, then when it was felt that the odds could get no higher, all of the inflated prices now available on the exchanges would have been snapped up to large stakes in one fell swoop. Someone, somewhere, had brought off a clever, but totally dishonest trade. They had been able to back the Derby favourite at way above its true odds, and many people had been gulled into laying it at unrealistic prices.

Of course history tells us that Yeats was eventually withdrawn from the Derby on the Thursday before Saturday's race due to a muscle injury. The clever coup just described had backfired on its instigators. Obviously one could say that the huge drift in price on 15 May might have been caused by the onset of the muscle injury, but this seems unlikely. No bulletin had been issued from Ballydoyle as early as this. The price had returned to its Saturday level by the following morning, and remained there for another fortnight before the horse was scratched. The more likely scenario is that a disinformation coup over Yeats had been pulled off on the weekend of 15 May. Even if the doubts about the participation of Yeats were genuine as early as that Saturday in May, then someone with very privileged information had not backed the horse, but laid it to huge sums, causing the drift in the market. Either way, the ordinary racing enthusiast using the exchanges had been taken for a ride.

The Yeats coup is an example of how unscrupulous gamblers can trick the markets when a horse's price drifts dramatically. In the opposite case, when there is a big drop in a horse's odds on the exchanges, it is important amid all the talk of meaningful positives and negatives from TV journalists, to avoid the trap of believing that every time a horse shortens in a big way, this is indicative of a stable gamble or represents a prospective coup by people in the know. In fact, it only takes a few biggish bets on the exchanges for the price to tumble as gullible punters jump on the bandwagon.

And what of ordinary punters who think they see an opportunity to do a little trading of their own? They naturally expect a big reduction in the odds when the computer screen shows large sums in line to back a horse. They cannot wait to take the available odds and back the horse with the intention of employing the manoeuvre explained in the introduction to this chapter, whereby they will be able to lay the horse back for a marginal profit once the weight of money forces the price down.

However, these large bets could just be dummies to get a lay order done. If the offers to back the horse for very large sums are suddenly withdrawn, then the odds will lengthen, not shorten. As a consequence the would-be trader, so far from being able to 'lock in' a profit, will be stranded with an unattractive bet at poor odds and no chance to redeem the situation.

Finally, the exchanges are open to exploitation by the most ruthless professionals of all in the betting jungle, for conventional bookmakers have begun to manipulate the exchange markets in their own favour. Bookmakers are barred from betting on the exchanges by their organisers, but the exchanges can do little about people acting on their behalf.

Now a basic manoeuvre by the bookmakers is to shorten up the price of a fancied horse by backing it heavily on the exchanges during the morning. This has a double purpose. First, the on-course bookmakers can open up their prices about animals so backed at much shorter prices than they would have been able to otherwise. And second, the fact that they themselves have backed a horse at a bigger price on the exchanges in the morning, and can lay it at a much shorter price on the racecourse, puts them into the classic trading position of backing a horse high and laying it low. They will make money from the horse whether it wins or loses. Again, it is the ordinary racing fan who suffers.

It has always been axiomatic that one will never make money from betting on horses by following the herd. The above examples of less than fair play underline the wisdom of this, and teach us an important lesson. Never take anything seen on an exchange website at complete face value, especially if it seems that easy money may not be too difficult to come by. Trickery, albeit within the rules of the game, is allowed in exchange betting, and everyone must be on their guard against it. Learn to read the signs, or you will discover that for every 'free lunch' that is apparently on offer there could well be a costly dinner to pay for.

10. Never Bet More Than You Can Afford To Lose On A Betting Exchange

The golden rule of all betting applies on the exchanges, only more so. There are many temptations lurking on betting-exchange websites for people sat at home in front of their PC. No cash is involved. All betting is on credit and one rush of blood to the head, one push of the wrong button, one unconsidered wrong move with the mouse can be very expensive. Higher odds than we have all been used to are frequently on offer. There is now the chance to pull out of a bad, pre-race bet by gambling in-running. Everyone has the right to be a layer, which some people seem to see, wrongly in this writer's view, as a sort of mini El Dorado.

If readers of this book can deal with all these new temptations in a sensible manner, and simultaneously keep their stakes within reasonable bounds, then these pages will not have been written in vain.

10
Bet with Method and Win

'Bet with method and WIN!' was the sales slogan of a betting magazine for which the author used to write in the 1960s and 1970s and which featured regular contributions from many of the best racing brains in the country at that time. The *Sporting Investor* is now, sadly, long defunct but its message lives on. Random betting does not pay; a methodical approach based on form and statistics gives the punter a fair chance of winning consistently.

The right psychology when it comes to betting is also an essential, without which nothing can be achieved. Perhaps the biggest single reason why most ordinary racing enthusiasts ultimately fail in their attempts to 'beat the book' is that they expect too much from their financial interest in racing. No sensible person would expect to thrive overnight in a commerical enterprise with just a small amount of capital invested. Why then do so many people, knowing full well the risks attached to backing horses, live in the constant hope of amassing a huge sum, for just a few pounds, in double-quick time?

The facile glamour which surrounds the 'Sport of Kings' may have much to do with it. Racing has always exuded an aura of apparently easy money which even the most hard-headed enthusiast finds difficult to resist, at least in the first instance. If racing is an activity where a lot of very rich men and women are prepared to spend thousands, even millions, for the pleasure of having their horses compete against one another, surely, the tyro says to himself or herself, it is not unreasonable to suppose that just a little of this excess of wealth will rub off on anyone spending some time in the serious study of the finer points of the sport.

However, racing is a hard school for all concerned and not least for those who bet on it. The favourite you backed, incredibly, finishes plumb last. An outsider which carries your cash is beaten in a photo finish. Very soon the dreams of easy pickings fade as fast as the winning burst of the 'certainty' in the big race you meant to back, but for some unaccountable reason did not. Racing is full of what might have been, for to err is human, and the sport has a way of extracting high penalties for the slightest mistake, or error of judgement.

As they learn more about the game, most level-headed people, although their enthusiasm remains undiminished in many cases, come to realise that racing is in fact a pastime, not the royal road to instant riches. Yet if horse racing is a hobby or a diversion, a 'great triviality' in a famous phrase, that does not mean it cannot, within reason, be a profitable one. The irrational hopes of vast wins for virtually nothing will almost certainly prove elusive, but this is not an argument that betting should not be organised along sound, businesslike lines.

A handsome payout from a limited outlay may be achievable from time to time, but any betting venture, even the most speculative, needs to be carefully planned, not merely in the context of a single day's racing, but in terms of a fairly prolonged series of wagers which may extend over an entire racing season or perhaps even longer.

There are four key elements in devising a winning strategy:

1 A sound method of selection or, more likely, several sound methods for different phases of the racing year, all ultimately working together towards the goal of a long-term profit.

2 A sensible method of staking either on single or multiple bets and, also, the willingness to take profits at appropriate times. No one can go on winning for ever, and 'giving winnings back to the bookie' is one of the worst failings of many punters.

3 An adequate betting bank that will see the punter comfortably to the end of a period of betting and afford the time and financial breathing space necessary to allow sound practice to pay off. Just as important, the betting bank should be sufficient to get the backer through those times when the going gets particularly tough. Here it generally pays to budget for the worst possible scenario.

4 The ability to learn from past mistakes and to modify betting procedures with a view to eliminating losing bets in the future. In this a complete record of all bets struck is a most valuable aid.

Backing horses, therefore, should never be regarded as a matter of pure chance, for much can be done to eliminate the element of luck in betting. The hit-and-miss punter who makes no plan and who simply hopes for the best will nearly always lose, and sooner rather than later. Anyone who is prepared to harness one or more of the formulae set out in this book to a controlled betting strategy must have reasonable prospects of making their pastime pay. Bookmakers treat horse racing as a business. So should you.

Index